THE PRE-RAPHAELITE BROTHERHOOD

THE PRE-RAPHAELITE BROTHERHOOD

NICK LOURAS

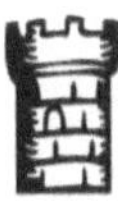

Published by Castle Imprint
www.castleimprint.com

First published 2026
Copyright © Nick Louras 2026

ISBN 978-1-7327399-3-2

To Kimberly, my wife.

CONTENTS

AUTHOR'S NOTE

I conceived this book as an inward turning spiral, or labyrinth, whereby the outer path of the early and late chapters trace the narrative history of the Pre-Raphaelite movement from its founding to its reception in the twentieth and twenty-first centuries, while the inner path of the central chapters provides analysis of symbolism and themes found in the paintings or poems themselves. In this way, I hope to provide a solid introduction for the casual admirer, while opening interesting lines of inquiry for the devotee.

P.R.B.

In the late summer or fall of 1848, John Everett Millais, Dante Gabriel Rossetti, and William Holman Hunt met to discuss their common interest in art. They had already begun this dialogue as students at the Royal Academy, and as members of a sketching circle, the Cyclographic Club. Nineteen year old Millais was by far the most accomplished, having entered the Royal Academy Schools in 1840, at the age of eleven. There he earned a string of prestigious prizes. Rossetti, a year older than Millais, but lacking his precocious talent, was still developing technique. His commitment to a career in the fine arts was often diverted by a calling to poetry. Nevertheless he studied painting first at Sass's Academy, then at the Royal Academy, before dropping out in March of 1848, to join the atelier of Ford Madox Brown. Holman Hunt was admitted to the Royal Academy Schools in 1844 on his third attempt. There he befriended Millais and with him shared certain frustrations with the way painting was taught.

Millais and Hunt believed that English art as practiced

under the auspices of the Academy was too often lax in detail, removed from nature, and clichéd in theme and composition. This they attributed to the rigid neoclassicism of the curriculum. The Academy's late founder, Sir Joshua Reynolds had, according to Hunt, "thought it expedient to take the Italian School at its proudest climax as a starting-point for English art."[1] Hunt believed that this focus deprived young artists of "the training that led to the making of Michelangelo."[2] Instead of learning to draw precisely from nature, students learned to repeat certain formulas and compositions.

The method of instruction practiced at the Academy came from the Mannerists of the Italian High Renaissance who learned by copying Raphael and, in turn, systematized Raphael's intensely personal style into a school of art. Even in nineteenth century England, Raphael's dramatic poses, dynamism, elongated and simplified forms, and distorted perspective were standards of narrative painting. Millais and Hunt believed this method to be entirely artificial, producing inferior copies of copies, deprived of the genius that had animated the original.

Hunt was quick to emphasize that "Pre-Raphaelitism is not Pre-Raphaelism." The genius of Raphael himself was not in question. Nor, for that matter, was the genius of Reynolds, who had been the preeminent portrait painter of his day. Reynolds is often remembered as a *bête noir* of the Pre-Raphaelites, but their objection was more to his pedagogy than his art. "The rules...which he loved so much to lay down were no fetters to him," Hunt wrote, "because he rose superior to them when his unbounded love of human nature was appealed to."[3] What they rejected was the notion that the genius of an artist or an art form could be broken down into certain axioms or stereotypes and thus learned by rote. Hunt's criticism of Reynolds and the Royal Academy was that the "independent genius of the first President could not be transmitted, but his binding rules were handed on."[4]

Neoclassicism had been the universal language of high art in Europe since the Renaissance. With its harmony, grandeur, and strict geometry, it had supplanted the more personal, decorative, variegated art of the Middle Ages. Medieval art had possessed its own universal language, gothic, but it also accommodated the vernacular. High art and low art were woven together with threads of mysticism, earthiness, Christian piety, color, abundance, light and darkness, strangeness, whimsy, mystery, transcendence. The strict organizing principle of classicism, for all its beauty and orthodoxy, rarely condescended to the vernacular, or touched the roots of a culture. The English gardens and family houses of the Georgian period are two fine examples of neoclassical vernacular.

Writing at the end of the nineteenth century, the French art critic Robert de la Sizeranne observed that, "Until 1848, one could admire art in England, but would not be surprised by it. Reynolds and Gainsborough were great masters, but they were eighteenth-century painters rather than eighteenth-century English painters. It was their models, their ladies and young girls, rather than brushwork, which gave an English character to their creations."[5] In looking back to an earlier art form it is clear that the Pre-Raphaelites were seeking a technique and aesthetic that would give expression to the English imagination. Hunt was unequivocal in later life, writing, "every student of art in the past was loyal to his own nationality, and that in these days men of British blood, whether of insular birth or of the homes beyond the seas, should not subject themselves to the influence of masters alien to the sentiments and principles of the great English poets and thinkers."[6] It was Rossetti more than either of the other founders of the Pre-Raphaelite movement who advanced Early Christian art as the vehicle for this sort of particularism.

In 1847 Holman Hunt had his painting, *The Eve of St Agnes* accepted by the jury for the Royal Academy Exhibition. At the show, Rossetti approached him, as Hunt later recalled, "repeating with emphasis his praise, and loudly declaring that my picture...was the best in the collection. Probably the fact that the subject was taken from Keats made him the more unrestrained, for I think no one had ever before painted any subject from this still little-known poet."[7] Hunt invited Rossetti to his studio where Hunt showed him his latest paintings and drawings. "I rejoiced to display [them] before a man of his poetic instincts," Hunt wrote, "and it was pleasant to hear him repeat my propositions and theories in his own richer phrase." He showed Rossetti a painting inspired by Edward Bulwer-Lytton's novel *Rienzi* in which Hunt was "putting in practice the principle of rejection of conventional dogma, and pursuing that of direct application to Nature for each feature."[8]

The seeds of the Pre-Raphaelite aesthetic were thus established before the three artists decided to form a group. The Brotherhood was founded at the house of Millais's parents in Gower Street near the British Museum. To their first meeting the young artists invited the writer William Michael Rossetti, Dante's younger brother, who was to be the chronicler and organizer of the group; Thomas Woolner, a sculptor; and the painters James Collinson and Frederic G. Stephens. It is unknown if the seven young men attempted to establish a credo or manifesto at their first meeting. They did produce a broad statement of principles:

1. To have genuine ideas to express.
2. To study nature attentively, so as to know how to express them.

3. To sympathize with what is direct and serious and heartfelt in previous art, to the exclusion of what is conventional and self-parading and learned by rote.
4. And most indispensable of all, to produce thoroughly good pictures and statues.[9]

This rather vague agenda suggests that at the beginning the Pre-Raphaelite Brotherhood lacked a uniform direction. The members had diverse approaches to art, varying depths of familiarity with art history, and unequal technical skills. They all, as William Rossetti noted, "belonged to the middle or lower-middle class of society."[10] None of them with the exception of William and Dante Rossetti had the kind of liberal education which included the study of Latin and Greek. During their monthly meetings, which were held with some regularity from late 1848 to the middle of 1850, they discussed their opinions on art with as much clarity as could be expected from individuals who were then just beginning to frame the general outlines of their practices. The most voluble of the three principle members, and the most adept at formulating his ideas, was Dante Gabriel Rossetti. He had, so his brother recalled, "an abundance of ideas, pictorial and also literary, and was fuller of 'notions' than" Millais or Hunt, with a "turn for proselytizing and 'pronunciamentos.'" He was the most defiant of the group, according to William, and, with a kind of adolescent verve, he held "art-sympathies highly developed in one direction, and unduly or even ignorantly restricted in others."[11]

At the first meeting of the Brotherhood, Millais exhibited a book of engravings that he kept in his studio. It contained poorly drawn reproductions of the frescoes at the Campo Santo in Pisa. Despite their limitations the engravings allowed the young artists to acquire some knowledge of fourteenth century Italian painting. This they supplemented with trips to the National Gallery, to view its collection of thirteenth and fourteenth century paintings, and no doubt by reading Anna Brownell Jameson's *Memoirs of the Early Italian Painters*, recently published in 1845.

Another volume that Millais shared with his colleagues was perhaps even more important to their project. This was a book of engravings by Joseph Ritter von Führich, illustrating the dramatic poem, *Life and Death of Saint Genevieve*, by the German Romantic poet, Ludwig Tieck. The medieval style and themes would have stirred the interest of all who attended the meeting. Von Führich was a member of a group of German painters who styled themselves, the Brotherhood of St Luke. They were known also as the Nazarenes. They established themselves in Rome in 1810, where, dressed in biblical costume, the "brothers" lived communally in an abandoned monastery. Like the nascent Pre-Raphaelite Brotherhood they abandoned neoclassicism for the aesthetics of the late Middle Ages and the early Renaissance. Although the Pre-Raphaelites did not formally pattern themselves after the Nazarenes, the influence of the latter on the former is visible in early Pre-Raphaelite drawings. Examples of this influence can be seen in Millais's *Two Lovers by a Rose Bush*, and Rossetti's drawing, *The First Anniversary of the Death of Beatrice*.

The three principle members of the newly formed Brotherhood began to prepare works for exhibition in 1849, Millais and Hunt at the Royal Academy, Rossetti at the Free Exhibition. Rossetti chose as his subject *The Girlhood of Mary Virgin*. None of the young artists had sufficient funds to hire models at this point so Rossetti turned to his mother, Frances, and sister, Christina, to sit for St Anne and the Virgin Mary, respectively. They modeled for him periodically at Holman Hunt's studio, which Rossetti shared. This working arrangement was fruitful, though it necessitated some measure of compromise. Hunt liked people around and Rossetti preferred solitude. Both profited from discussions on art and pursued their goals independently.

For his piece, Hunt completed the scene from Bulwer-Lytton that he had earlier previewed for Rossetti, titled, *Rienzi vowing to obtain justice for the death of his young brother, slain in a skirmish between the Colonna and the Orsini factions*. Hunt's composition followed a tradition of heroic battlefield death scenes established in the eighteenth century by Benjamin West in his *Death of General Wolfe*.

Millais was the second of the group to try his hand at illustrating a scene from the poetry of John Keats. His painting, *Lorenzo and Isabella*, was an adaptation of Keats's poem *Isabella, or the Pot of Basil*, itself an adaptation of a story from Boccaccio's *Decameron*. Both poems concern a young woman from a wealthy family, Isabella, who falls in love with one of her brothers' retainers, Lorenzo. Her brothers, who plan to marry her to a rich man, learn of the romance. They lure the hapless Lorenzo to an out-of-the-way place, and there, murder him. Lorenzo appears to Isabella in a dream and leads her to his body. She digs it up and cuts off the head, which she plants in a pot of basil. Watered by her tears, the plant thrives. Her brothers grow suspicious and steal the pot, only to discover the rotting head of their victim. Horrified by what they have done the brothers leave Florence in self-imposed exile. Isabella, having lost both her lover and the solace of the pot of basil, descends into madness and dies.

For his painting, Millais chose to depict the moment that the brothers become aware of the romance. The scene is set around a table, at which Isabella, her brothers, and their guests are dining. Lorenzo is seated beside Isabella. He offers her a blood orange, cut in half, as if to foreshadow his own severed head, while the brothers watch from across the table. There are two focal points in the composition. The first is the young couple: Lorenzo, bowing to offer his plate, regarding his lover with gentle, even reverential concern, but also conspiracy and the hardness of resolve; Isabella, accepting the orange, but looking down, aware of the danger, resisting the urge to acknowledge him, her body tense with the effort of self-denial. The other focal point is one of her brothers, seated in the fore-ground, across from them. He is an extraordinary, brutish char-acter, leaning forward to kick a dog who cowers in Isabella's lap. In an outstretched hand he cracks a nut with a levered nutcracker.

Curator Carol Jacobi, in a 2012 essay on the painting, draws attention to a shadow cast on the table by the brother's arm. It appears to rise diagonally from his groin in the place of a phal-lus. Jacobi connects this to the "salt cellar spilling its contents," which, together with the "shadow and groin," she describes as "an unambiguous equivalent for ejaculation."[12] Millais has created a sort of moral illustration, contrasting these two models of manhood: the chaste, modest, chivalrous Lorenzo with the vulgar, murderous, and sexually incontinent brother.

All three paintings revealed a medieval influence, whether in subject matter (Hunt's *Rienzi*), style (Rossetti's *Virgin*), or both (Millais's *Isabella*). Rossetti in particular captured elements reminiscent of an altarpiece in his domestic scene. Despite the ambiguousness of their initial statement, the clear meaning of the Brotherhood's name was reflected in each contribution.

The initials P.R.B. appended to the signatures of Millais, Hunt, and Rossetti, apparently went unnoticed on the paint-ings they exhibited at the Royal Academy and elsewhere in 1849. This was not the case the following year when they caught the attention of Charles Dickens. The meaning of the enigmatic letters had been revealed to the public before the opening of the Royal Academy show. On May 4, 1850 a columnist, who was not an art critic, wrote in the *Illustrated London News*, that for those confused by the letters P.R.B., the secret was that they stood for the Pre-Raphaelite Brotherhood, a group of "ingenious gentlemen who profess themselves practitioners of Early Christian Art."[13] Dickens wrote a scathing critique of the Pre-Raphaelite paintings for his journal, *Household Words*. In the edition of June 15, 1850, Dickens began his review of the annual Royal Academy show with a warning: "You will have the goodness to discharge from your minds all Post-Raphael ideas, all religious aspirations, all elevating thoughts, all tender, awful, sorrowful, ennobling, sacred, graceful, or beautiful associations, and to prepare yourselves... for the lowest depths of what is mean, odious, repulsive, and revolting."[14]

The target of this criticism was a painting by Millais, *Christ in the House of His Parents*. As the title suggests, the work depicts a scene from the boyhood of Jesus. The setting is Joseph's workshop, which Millais based on a real carpenter's shop on Oxford Street in London. The composition is rich in Christian symbolism. Jesus has cut his hand on a nail. Blood runs from the center of his palm to the foot beneath it, prefiguring the wounds of the crucifixion. The Virgin Mary kneels before him, as though at the foot of the cross. A young John the Baptist brings water to clean the wound, foreshadowing his baptism of Christ. A white dove, the symbol of the Holy Spirit, watches from a ladder in the background. A triangle on the wall above Christ's head suggests the Trinity. Outside a flock of sheep is gathered, anticipating his mission as shepherd of men.

If Dickens saw any of this he did not recognize it. He accused Millais of portraying the savior as "a hideous, wry-necked, blubbering, red-headed boy," and the Virgin Mary as a "Monster" who would stand out "in her ugliness" from the company of "the vilest cabaret in France, or the lowest ginshop in England." Sweeping the rest of the company into his critique, he wrote, "Wherever it is possible to express ugliness of feature, limb, or attitude, you have it expressed."[15]

When we look at the painting today we see none of the depravity that Dickens portrays. The religious subject is treated with reverence. The figures are rendered with great tenderness. The naturalism, though striking, was hardly novel, having a precedence going back to Caravaggio. What could possibly have elicited such contempt?

Dickens was clearly reacting to something other than the technical merits of the painting when he wrote his review. We do not have to search far to learn what that was: Dickens found the notion of a backward-looking art movement plainly ridiculous. He compared the Pre-Raphaelite Brotherhood to a hypothetical "Pre-Newtonian Brotherhood" for those who objected to being bound by the laws of gravity, a "Pre-Galileo Brotherhood" for those who "refuse[d] to perform any annual revolution round the Sun," a "Pre-Gower and Pre-Chaucer Brotherhood" for those who would revive the old idiosyncratic English spellings, or a "Pre-Laurentians Brotherhood" for those who would abolish printed books in favor of painstakingly copied manuscripts.[16]

Dickens may have been influenced by the writer in the *Illustrated* news a month earlier, who had interpreted the Pre-Raphaelite Project in a mocking tone. The artists, he wrote, having embraced "Early Christian Art," over and against "the Medieval Schools of Italy," now "devote their energies to saints, squeezed out perfectly flat."[17] Both writers seem to imply a conscious rejection of technical progress in draftsmanship on the part of the young artists, to comic effect. Was this new school of painting going to deprive itself of the knowledge of proper proportion and perspective out of willful pride? Perhaps Dickens could not resist making the joke. But an open-minded look at the paintings might have shown him otherwise.

Holman Hunt's contribution to the Royal Academy exhibition was intended as a companion piece to Millais's, and was, in composition, even more ambitious. The subject, and title, was, *A Converted British Family Sheltering a Christian Missionary from the Persecution of the Druids*. In the foreground Hunt depicted the interior of a simple wooden fisherman's shed on a riverbank, where the titular missionary has collapsed into the arms of the mother of the family, while the men guard the door, and the children succor him. In the background, seen in part through the windows at the top of the hut, a mob of pagans, commanded by a Druid priest, chase down a second missionary to his inevitable martyrdom. Although the scene has its own dramatic narrative and tension, Hunt's composition suggests an episode from the Gospels: the Deposition of Christ, when the Savior's body was lowered from the cross. Here the postures of the missionary and the woman holding him from behind clearly evoke the *Pietà*, the traditional artistic representation of Mary cradling the body of Jesus. On the wall above them is a red cross roughly drawn by the persecuted Christians for their worship. One of the daughters removes a thorn from the missionary's robe, representing the crown of thorns, while another prepares to bathe his face with sponge and water.

Exhibited together, the relationship between Hunt's painting, and Millais's *Christ in the House of His Parents*, would have been readily apparent. Both works depicted a primitive Christianity. Both employed traditional, iconographic details. In portraying scenes from Christian history before and after the crucifixion, both placed Christ's passion at the center of the narrative. Hunt judged his painting to be among the best of his own work. Appraising it more than two decades later, he wrote to Edward Lear, "sometimes when I look at the Early Xtians I feel rather ashamed that I have got no further than later years have brought me, but the truth is that at twenty—health, enthusiasm and yet unpunished confidence in oneself carries a man very near his ultimate length of tether."[18]

Both Hunt and Rossetti had benefitted in their education from a trip to the Continent in the fall of 1849. They visited France and Belgium. In Paris they toured the large public galleries, studying canvases by Titian, da Vinci, Veronese, and van Dyck. At the Louvre they were awestruck by *The Coronation of the Virgin* by Fra Angelico, which was, according to Hunt, "of peerless grace and sweetness in the eyes of us both."[19] In Antwerp they admired the paintings of the Early Netherlandish artists, Jan van Eyck and Hans Memling, foremost. They were prepared for their encounter with the brilliant, detailed works of the Early Netherlandish painters, having already studied van Eyck's 1434 work, *Portrait of Giovanni Arnolfini and his Wife*, at the National Gallery. It was the graphic quality, almost brittle composition, and absence of free, painterly brush strokes in the paintings by van Eyck and his followers that became the goal of Hunt and Rossetti for their own works.

Of all the paintings exhibited by members of the Brotherhood in 1850, the most influential on the development of Pre-Raphaelite style and technique, was Rossetti's *Ecce Ancilla Domini (The Annunciation)*, shown at the National Institution, formerly the Free Exhibition. The painting had begun with a preliminary sketch in late November of 1849. This process was recorded by Rossetti's brother William in his journal. He described the work-in-progress as depicting the Virgin in bed, "without any bedclothes on, an arrangement which may be justified in consideration of the hot climate, and the Angel Gabriel is to be presenting a lily to her."[20] The painting was to be almost entirely white, with contained uses of one color at a time: a red embroidery in the foreground, a blue curtain in the background, yellow halos, a window opened on a blue sky.

In mid-December, Rossetti began to paint the Virgin's head, using his sister Christina as a model, and later in the month drew the head of the Angel, with his brother William modeling. By mid-January he was busy working on the drapery and in early February had moved on to the red cloth embroidery in the foreground. On March 29, William recorded that his brother had painted the feet and arm of the Angel from a model, had another, Miss Love, sit for the Virgin's hair, and a third to finish the Angel's head. The execution was a protracted process as Rossetti, now working in the studio of Ford Madox Brown, struggled to achieve the level of technical mastery possessed by his colleagues. The finished product was a painting of exceptional tenderness and beauty, in some ways less mature than Hunt's or Millais's work, but in others, particularly the figure of the Virgin, entirely developed.

With this painting Rossetti introduced what would become a signature Pre-Raphaelite technique. Whereas most artists prepared their canvases with a coat of neutral, solid color, called a toned ground, Rossetti painted his canvas bright white. By applying the colors over this white ground in almost transparent glazes, the effect was to make the picture seem illuminated. Beginning in 1850 both Millais and Hunt adopted the same practice, amplifying its effect by using a wet white ground. Millais used the technique to depict sunlight on faces in his painting, *The Woodsman's Daughter*, completed the following year. Its application can be seen to great advantage in Hunt's adaptation of Shakespeare's *Two Gentlemen of Verona*, titled, *Valentine Rescuing Sylvia from Proteus*, also completed in

1851. In this painting particularly, Hunt achieved an almost preternatural effect of light.

Experimentation with color had been an ongoing interest of all three artists. Hunt recalled a visit to the Royal Academy by the painter Claude Lorraine Nursey during one of Hunt's first terms there. Nursey had given a lecture and then stayed to watch the students work. At the time Hunt was copying Sir David Wilkie's painting, *The Blind Fiddler*. Nursey had once been a pupil of Wilkie and explained the latter's practice of applying all his paint, whether for a section of a painting or an entire work, in one sitting. In this way he never painted over dried paint, as most artists did, which tended to dull the colors. For Hunt this had been a revelation. "I tried the method," he wrote, "and I now looked at all paintings with the question whether they had been so executed. I began to trace the purity of work in the quattrocentists to the drilling of undeviating manipulation with which fresco-painting had furnished them, and I tried to put aside the loose, irresponsible handling to which I had been trained, and which was nearly universal at the time, and to adopt the practice which excused no false touch."[21] Hunt seems to have arrived at the technique that he used in *Valentine Rescuing Sylvia* by combining the innovations of Rossetti and Wilkie. By painting on a *wet* white ground he was able to achieve more luminous colors even than Rossetti had, but only because he had rigorously adopted Wilkie's constraints. As Hunt observed, "Painting of this kind cannot be retouched except with an entire loss of luminosity."[22]

Millais had been experimenting with similar methods around this same time. Hunt remembered both Millais and himself arriving at the use of a wet white ground independent of one another. This would seem to suggest that the various influences that informed the technique were being discussed among the members of the Brotherhood during their meetings leading up to the various individual applications. Once it had been perfected, Millais proposed that they should keep the process "as a precious secret"[23] amongst themselves, which they did. When Millais and Hunt revealed the secret to Ford Madox Brown, years later, Brown recognized it as a technique of the early-Renaissance fresco painters. According to Hunt, Brown "enlarged on the mystery as nothing less than the secret of the old masters, who thus secured the transparency and solidity...valued so much in fresco, the wet white half dry forming an equivalent to the moist intonaco grounds upon which the master had to do his painting of that day while the surface was still humid."[24]

While the Pre-Raphaelites worked on their paintings for the 1850 exhibition, discussion at their meetings centered around the publication of a literary journal, intended to circulate the ideas and aesthetics of the group. The first issue of *The Germ* appeared on January 1, 1850. The title was an expression of the Brotherhood's commitment to honor nature down to the smallest detail—the germ, the seed—but also of their creative aspiration: it was the germ of an idea and a movement.

The inaugural issue contained essays; reviews; poems by Thomas Woolner, Ford Madox Brown, Dante, William, and Christina Rossetti; and an etching by Holman Hunt to illustrate Woolner's poem, "My Beautiful Lady." It is not surprising that the Rossetti siblings dominated the contents of the journal. They belonged to a multigenerational literary family of mixed Italian and English stock. Their father, Gabriele Pasquale Rossetti, was an exiled Dante scholar. He taught the Italian language at King's College London. Their maternal uncle was John Polidori, the physician and confidante of Lord Byron. Dr Polidori had created the modern vampire genre with his short story, "The Vampyre," written on a challenge from Lord Byron to compose a ghost story. That same challenge, issued to Byron's guests one evening at the Villa Diodati in Switzerland, inspired Mary Shelley to write *Frankenstein*.

The Rossetti household revolved around the study of Dante, Petrarch, and other early Italian writers and was often full of émigré scholars. Dante Gabriel was immersed in the life of his namesake and like his father would contribute to the corpus of literature on medieval Italian poetry. A fourth sibling, Maria, later wrote her own volume on Dante.

The children enjoyed a happy childhood. They were baptized in the Church of England and educated at home by their parents, learning from the Bible, St Augustine, *Pilgrim's Progress*, the English classics, pedagogical novels, and fairy tales. The bohemian family, though highly cultured, was never financially secure. When health problems forced Gabriele Rossetti to step down from his professorship at King's College in 1843, much of the burden of supporting the household fell on the children. Christina was often left alone during this time and suffered bouts of depression and weak health, though she found catharsis in Christianity and in poetry. Like her mother and sister, Christina became involved in the Oxford Movement of the Church of England. Her faith permeated her writing. Biographer Lona Mosk Packer cites "the Bible, hagiographies, folk and fairy tales" as her first influences.[25] Christina's best known poem, "In Bleak Midwinter," is sung as a Christmas carol in Anglican churches to this day.

The two poems that Christina Rossetti contributed to *The Germ* stand out in their maturity. At this point she was already an accomplished poet, having published work in the *Athenaeum*. "Dream Land" contains a nimble, subtle interweaving of her influences, at once evoking the enchanted slumber of a sleeping princess from fable, and the soul of the dead awaiting the resurrection of the body. In this, her verse achieves a melancholy beauty:

> Rest, rest, a perfect rest,
>> Shed over brow and breast;
>> Her face is toward the west,
>> The purple land.
>> She cannot see the grain
>> Ripening on hill and plain;
>> She cannot feel the rain
>> Upon her hand.[26]

The sadness that permeates her early poems may have reflected an emotional state that Christina experienced, though it was also perfectly characteristic of Victorian late-romantic verse. Her second contribution to the inaugural issue of *The Germ*, titled, "An End," is no less mournful.

In reading through the four numbers of *The Germ* one is struck by the consistency of approach and subject matter in the poetry. The verse represents an extension of the Brotherhood's artistic preference for biblical and medieval themes. James Collinson wrote a long poem, "The Child Jesus," published in the second number. It was influenced by Millais' picture, *Christ in the House of His Parents*. Collinson's description of the cottages overlooking the sea in Nazareth where the Holy Family lived is quite lovely:

> A honeysuckle and a moss-rose grew,
>> With many blossoms, on their cottage front;
>> And o'er the gable warmed by the South
>> A sunny grape vine broadened shady leaves
>> Which gave its tendrils shelter, as they hung
>> Trembling upon the bloom of purple fruit.[27]

In the same issue, the poem "Morning Sleep," by William Bell Scott, an art teacher and friend of Rossetti, combined images of nature with Arthurian legend. When the contribution was submitted, William Michael Rossetti described it as "gloriously fine." One verse reads:

The spell
    Of Merlin old that ministered to fate,
    The tales of visiting ghosts, or fairy elves,
    Or witchcraft, are no fables. But his task
    Is ended with the night;—the thin white moon
    Evades the eye, the sun breaks through the trees,
    And the charmed wizard comes forth a mere man
    From out his circle.[28]

The Germ was not a success in its own time. Only 70 copies from an initial print run of 700 were sold. There were fewer readers of the second issue published on January 30, and still fewer for the third and fourth, published in March and April, respectively. The expenses of this venture were too onerous for the ambitious, though virtually penniless, artists to bear, and the support of their better-heeled friends was soon exhausted. After four issues the enterprise folded. Although *The Germ* was not a breakthrough for the Brotherhood it remains a vital record of its ideas in their earliest phase, and was reprinted several times beginning in the late nineteenth century, when the Pre-Raphaelites had achieved greater fame.

The subject matter of the Pre-Raphaelite pictures varied from artist to artist but clear commonalities were visible by the time they had submitted their works for exhibition in 1851. In addition to shared techniques, the artists shared a preference, though not exclusive, for biblical and medieval themes over classical and mythological, for character and *mise-en-scène* over landscape, and for bright color over the popular preference for smoky browns. Within this broad consensus was a great range of influences. Rossetti was particularly fascinated with Dante and medieval devotional art; Holman Hunt with biblical themes; Millais was more or less encyclopaedic in his references, sometimes turning to Shakespeare, at other times contemporary daily life, the Bible, English history, or contemporary Regency and Victorian poetry.

Millais produced three pictures for the Royal Academy show in 1851: *Mariana, The Return of the Dove to the Arc,* and *The Woodsman's Daughter.* The first was taken from a poem by Alfred, Lord Tennyson based on Shakespeare's *Measure for Measure.* In Millais's rendering, the character of Mariana looks plaintively out of large gothic windows. She has been rejected as a bride because of the loss of her dowry in a shipwreck. The caption to the picture is from Tennyson's 1830 poem:

She only said, 'My life is dreary, / He cometh not,' she said; / She said, 'I am aweary, aweary, / I would that I were dead!'[29]

Tennyson was a particular favorite of the Pre-Raphaelites. Undoubtedly the finest English poet of his generation, Tennyson had been appointed Poet Laureate in 1850, with the support of Prince Albert, an early admirer. The same year Tennyson published "In Memoriam," a tribute to his late friend Arthur Henry Hallam. The work was a sensation. William Rossetti, as a reviewer for *The Spectator,* received an advance copy. Upon reading it he rushed home and passed the book to his brother. Although it was after midnight Dante read the entire poem aloud. Thereafter the Pre-Raphaelites hung on Tennyson's every word, illustrating many of his works, most notably episodes from his tales of King Arthur.

Lord Tennyson spent most of his career as a poet in the

realm of Arthurian legend. It was not by any means his only subject, but it was one to which he returned again and again. His definitive treatment of the rise and fall of Camelot, the book-length cycle, *Idylls of the King*, was written over a quarter of a century between 1859 and 1885. But much earlier, at the outset of his career, Tennyson identified the unrealized potential in this important British mythology, writing that, "most of the big things except 'King Arthur' had been done."[30]

Previous generations of Romantic poets had consciously rejected the subject. "As to Arthur...What have we to do with him," asked Coleridge.[31] Lord Byron was likewise disinterested. "By the by," he wrote, "I fear that Sir Tristem and Sir Lancelot were no better than they should be...So much for chivalry. Burke need not have regretted that its days are over." [32] Yet Tennyson dared to assert the relevancy of the Arthurian tradition to the modern world, and in so doing, achieved not only a masterpiece, but a renewal of the Victorian imagination.

Tennyson first read Sir Thomas Malory's fifteenth-century prose epic, *Le Morte d'Arthur*, in his youth. "The vision of Arthur as I have drawn him," he later told his son, "came upon me when, little more than a boy, I first lighted upon Malory."[33] Tennyson understood the character as "a man who spent himself in the cause of honour, duty and self-sacrifice, who felt and aspired with his nobler knights, though with a stronger and clearer conscience than any of them."[34]

It was not immediately clear to Tennyson how to approach the subject. In the 1830s he wrote four different poems that dealt with Arthur and Camelot in various ways. He also experimented with treatments and arrangements of the material in four outlines written during the same period.

The outlines were composed in the early 1830s, probably around 1833. The first describes the landscape of Camelot in prose, focusing on the mountain where Arthur's hall was built:

"The Mount was the most beautiful in the world...but all underneath it was hollow, and the mountain trembled...and there ran a prophecy that the mountain and the city on some wild morning would topple into the abyss and be no more."[35] The second outline records the symbolism that the young Tennyson attributed to various characters: Mordred, the skeptical understanding; Merlin, science; the Round Table, liberal institutions; Excalibar, war.[36] Another outline arranges the cast of characters based on their relationships to one another. The last is a proposed sequence for a five-act narrative connecting the legends. While none of these early sketches exactly predicted the form that Tennyson's mature work would take, they give a sense of the systematic approach he used to arrive at it.

The most famous of the poems from this period was *The Lady of Shalott*. It tells the story of a cursed woman who lives in isolation, weaving images of the world she sees reflected in a mirror, until a glimpse of the knight Lancelot compels her to venture into the world, even though it will mean her doom. The poem was based on a medieval Italian novelette from the thirteenth century collection, *Cento Novelle Antiche*. Tennyson was, at the time, unfamiliar with Malory's version of the tale and later said, "I doubt whether I should ever have put it in that shape if I had been then aware of the Maid of Astolat in *Mori Arthur*."[37] The subtext in Tennyson's rendering is the movement of the artist from isolation and imitation of the world into experience of the world—in Tennyson's words, "out of the region of shadows into that of realities."[38] To develop this theme, Tennyson modified the story substantially. Several important elements, like the Lady's mirror, are his invention, not present in the original source.

The other three poems were *Sir Launcelot and Queen Guinevere*, *Sir Galahad*, and the *Morte d'Arthur*. In all of them

Tennyson pays close attention to imagery, often expanding upon depictions in Malory's narrative for heightened emphasis. For example, he turns Malory's fairly straightforward image of Excalibur as a sword decorated with precious stones into a sword that "twinkled with diamond studs, / Myriads of topaz-lights, and jacinth-work / Of subtlest jewellery."[39] But he also drew out and expanded the interior life of the characters. The dramatic last words that Tennyson gives to Arthur, while of his own invention, add to Malory rather than contradicting him. The emphasis of Arthur's speech in the *Morte d'Arthur* is on prayer; Arthur says, "More things are wrought by prayer / Than this world dreams of."[40] The entire speech reflects Tennyson's skill at weaving his own moral vision into a poem that remains relatively faithful to the source material.

By the 1840s Tennyson had found in King Arthur a figure who could represent idealism and faith for Victorian society. His early experimentations would bear fruit in the *Idylls of the King*. In that work Tennyson navigated the knife's edge between the heroic and tragic, achieving something sublime. In the end Arthur slays the traitor Mordred in battle but is left "all but slain himself," his kingdom fallen.[41] As in Malory, he is last seen taken by boat toward the mythical island of Avalon, "Somewhere far off, pass[ing] on and on, and go[ing] / From less to less and vanish[ing] into light." To cite Tennyson's own early symbolism: faith and virtue overcome materialism and doubt, but not without a cost. And indeed, the Victorian faith —Tennyson's own faith—was even then retreating into mystery and mysticism. But this was not a final retreat. Arthur is an inherently Christlike figure, destined to "come again / To rule once more." The Idylls end with another beginning: "And the new sun rose bringing the new year."[42]

All three of Millais's pictures in the Royal Academy show of 1851 were accomplished with deftness of drawing, flatness of surface, and minimal use of modeling in the three dimensional forms. The same may be said of Holman Hunt's submission, *Valentine Rescuing Sylvia from Proteus*. Hunt drew his subject from the climax of *Two Gentlemen of Verona*. In Shakespeare's early comedy, Valentine and Proteus both love Silvia, though her heart belongs to Valentine. After rescuing her from outlaws, Proteus threatens to rape Silvia, if she will not consent to love him. Valentine intervenes. Proteus repents and gives his love to Julia who has disguised herself as his page boy.

Reviewing Hunt's adaptation for *The Spectator*, the Rossetti brothers were, of course, effusive, calling it, "the finest we have seen from its painter." Dante drew the reader's attention to the two female figures. Silvia, he wrote, "nestles to her strong knight, rescued and secure; while poor Julia leans, sick to swooning, against a tree, and tries with a trembling hand to draw the ring from her finger. Both these figures are truly creations, for the very reason that they are appropriate individ-ualities, and not self-seeking idealisms."[43] William used much of the column to rebuke the hanging committee of the Royal Academy for its poor job in highlighting such an important work.

The paintings of the Pre-Raphaelites and their associates at the Royal Academy show of 1851 received largely negative reviews. The critic of *The Times* condemned them for "the puerility or infancy of their art," their "monkish style" and "monkish follies." A "morbid infatuation" with ancient art, had, he wrote, caused them to sacrifice "truth, beauty, and genuine feeling to mere eccentricity."[44] Clearly Charles Dickens had set the tone and terms of public debate in his review of the previous year. Detractors of the new movement shared a common rhetoric and a few common points of opposition.

The seemingly impenetrable wall of critical resistance to

the Pre-Raphaelite Brotherhood would soon break, however, with the emergence of an extraordinary ally. John Ruskin was a formidable art critic whose opinions held great weight among both scholars and collectors. The first two volumes of his monumental work, *Modern Painters*, had been published between 1843 and 1846. In them, Ruskin laid the philosophical groundwork for an art closer to nature. He idealized medieval and Renaissance art in terms of the convergence of truth, beauty, and religion. Ruskin argued that the job of the artist was to convey "truth to nature," by which he meant "moral as well as material truth."[45] By this measure he judged the contemporary landscape painter J.M.W. Turner to be the greatest artist who ever worked in that field, elevating him above the Old Masters of the Baroque period. He was deeply critical of contemporary historical painters who, he wrote, were "permitted to pander more fatally every year to the vicious English taste, which can enjoy nothing but what is theatrical, entirely unchastised, nay, encouraged and lauded by the very men who endeavor to hamper our great landscape painters with rules derived from consecrated blunders."[46] Here was the very language that the young Pre-Raphaelites were using to articulate their dissatisfaction with the prevailing wisdom of the Academy. If anyone could understand the aims of the Brotherhood, they had to hope it would be Ruskin. Indeed, his defense, when it came, was swift, authoritative, and generous.

On May 13, 1851, *The Times* published a signed letter from Ruskin expressing "regret" that the "tone" of the paper's critique of the Pre-Raphaelite paintings had been "scornful as well as severe." He wrote that the "labour bestowed on those works, and their fidelity to a certain order of truth (labour and fidelity which are altogether indisputable) ought at once to have placed them above the level of mere contempt." He insisted that the young artists were "at a turning point, from which they may either sink into nothingness or rise to very real greatness."[47] On May 30, Ruskin followed up with a second letter, in which he concluded that the Pre-Raphaelites, "may, as they gain experience, lay in our land the foundations of a school of art nobler than has been seen for three hundred years."[48] With these words the fortunes of the members of the Brotherhood changed forever.

The Pre-Raphaelites were emerging as integral drivers of the medieval artistic revival that would come to define the Victorian age, largely thanks to the advocacy of two men: Ruskin and His Royal Highness Prince Albert.

The same year that Ruskin penned his defense of the Pre-Raphaelites he published the first volume in his study of Venetian gothic architecture, *The Stones of Venice*. Here he began to lay out a philosophy of gothicism over and against the prevailing classicism. In subsequent volumes he would elaborate on this philosophy, defining six characteristic elements of gothic design: savageness, changefulness, naturalism, grotesqueness, rigidity, and redundance. Ruskin wrote with irresistible enthusiasm, praising gothic ornament for its "prickly independence, and frosty fortitude, jutting into crockets, and freezing into pinnacles; here starting up into a monster, there germinating into a blossom; anon knitting itself into a branch, alternately thorny, bossy, and bristly, or writhed into every form of nervous entanglement; but even when most graceful, never for an instant languid, always quickset; erring, if at all, ever on the side of brusquerie."[49] This was not the language of archeology. Ruskin was not describing relics or museum pieces. In his poetic prose he conjured a vital, living, irrepressible art form.

No one did more to midwife that art form than Prince Albert. When he married Queen Victoria in 1840 the young

German prince became an influential patron and advocate for the arts in Britain. One of his first official duties was to lead the Royal Commission tasked with designing the interior of the new Houses of Parliament. He brought to this appointment a vision entirely sympathetic with the gothic Berry-Pugin architecture. The Prince possessed an informed taste for medieval and medieval-revival aesthetics. He collected everything from Tuscan *trecento* primitives to contemporary German romantic painters. Under his guidance, Clare Willsdon writes, "the wall-painting, sculpture, and stained glass used as a matter of course by the medieval builders" were adopted for the new building.[50] Prince Albert advised the artist William Dyce to draw from Arthurian legend for the murals of the Queen's Robing Room. Albert's own Lutheran culture, which had not needed to contend with either iconoclasm or the gaudy Baroque influence of the counter-reformation, may have contributed to his easy familiarity with the gothic style.

To a certain extent the Prince became involved in arts and culture because he lacked a formal outlet for his talents. Parliament had been opposed to granting any political power to a foreign prince. Not only was he denied the title of King Consort, he was also denied peerage and military rank. Although in time he did take on responsibility for the affairs of state, it is a credit to his genius that, for most of his short career, he had a greater influence on British culture than almost any other man of his age, despite having little practical power.

Beginning in 1850, the Prince, together with members of the Royal Society for the Encouragement of Arts, Manufactures, and Commerce, organized what would be the first World's Fair. The Great Exhibition, as it was known, opened in 1851 in the Kensington district of London, housed within a custom-built "Crystal Palace" of cast-iron, steel, and glass, large enough to enclose full-grown trees. The exhibition showcased rich displays of traditional culture and ultra-modern technology side by side. Visitors encountered the Koh-i-Noor diamond from India and the Daria-i-Noor from Persia; a stuffed elephant bedecked in the livery and howdah of an Indian rajah; porcelain, tapestries, and silk from France; decorative arts, furs, sledges, and Cossack armor from Russia; an Egyptian Court with towering statues and pillars, mummies, and antiquities. At the same time they could marvel at Stevenson's hydraulic press, adding machines, a state-of-the-art printing press, folding pianos, carriages, and velocipedes.

To represent Britain in this grand evocation of the Victorian future, Prince Albert invited A.W.N. Pugin to create a Medieval Court. Pugin had previously collaborated with Sir Charles Berry on the gothic revival design of the new Houses of Parliament. He was now in the last year of his life. This would be his swan song, what Paul Atterbury called, "his final consuming project."[51] Pugin designed stained glass, furniture, sculpture, and textiles in the gothic revival style. He had these fabricated by the various firms of craftsmen with whom he had long collaborated, in what Jeffrey Auerbach describes as a "preview of the team-oriented craftsmanship that would characterize William Morris's Arts and Crafts productions."[52] The effect was to create a fanciful immersive experience into an imagined realm.

The Queen's Gallery[53] at Buckingham Palace hosted a superlative exhibition in 2010, entitled, *Victoria & Albert: Art & Love.* The exhibition brought together works commissioned and collected by the royal couple. To be in the midst of a collection so vast and personal was to be brought into a sort of rare proximity to Victoria and her age. One of the revelations of this exhibition was the extent to which the royal couple not only encouraged but guided the development of British and European art in the nineteenth century.

Queen Victoria and her husband Prince Albert were passionate in their patronage of the arts. The contemporary painter William Powell Frith observed that their "treatment of artists displayed a gracious kindness delightful to experience." [54] They both had substantial training in the field. Queen Victoria had received drawing lessons for almost ten years from Richard Westall, a Royal Academician famous for his portraits of Lord Byron. She subsequently learned oil and watercolor technique from the Scottish landscape painter William Leighton Leitch, with whom she studied for over twenty years.

For his own part, Prince Albert was among the best-educated patrons of his day. As explained in the curatorial notes for *Art & Love*,

> [His Royal Highness] belonged to the first generation of students to hear lectures in the new discipline of Art History. Visiting Italy as a nineteen-year-old he had steeped himself in Renaissance painting and made contact with leading scholars, many of them German expatriates. Ludwig Gruner, an engraver from Dresden famous for his prints after Raphael, became the Prince's artistic adviser in 1842. Gruner acquired for Prince Albert twenty-seven Italian pictures of the kind then known as 'Primitives'... [55]

The Prince was an avid collector of medieval and Renaissance art, and a champion of modern practitioners of the style, including the painter William Dyce, to whom he awarded the commission to paint the interior of the Palace of Westminster. Frith's daughter, Jane Ellen Panton, recalled that, "[Albert] honestly loved art for art's sake, and...did more for artists than any king or prince ever did before or since."[56]

The royal couple often met artists and visited their studios in person, an unusual practice for royalty. They were known to offer frank critiques and even suggestions. Frith commented on their extensive knowledge. He was specifically impressed by Albert's ability to discuss the composition, light, and shading of a painting. Frith afterwards followed some of Albert's suggestions, as did the painter John Martin, who affirmed that they were thoughtful, valuable, and reflected well on the Prince's understanding of art.

Victoria cannily worked with Franz Xaver Winterhalter and other court painters to portray the royal family in such a way as to reflect both the Queen's political supremacy and the Prince's authority as *pater familias*. From the same curatorial notes:

Queen Victoria was the first Queen Regnant, and Prince Albert the first male consort, since the early 1700s. This presented a challenge to portrait painters, since the conventions that had been appropriate for Victoria's male predecessors no longer applied.

Winterhalter looked for inspiration to the Dutch and Flemish old masters, especially Van Dyck, but his Royal Family in 1846 was a brilliant and original response to the challenge. The viewer is left in no doubt that the Queen and her eldest son represent the royal line, while Prince Albert rules the family.

Winterhalter's family picture quickly became famous through public exhibition and engraving.[57]

It was not only the traditional arts which attracted royal attention and patronage. Prince Albert was interested in how art could be related to manufacturing, making practical items beautiful, and beautiful items available to a broader section of the public. He wanted to encourage the development of good taste even among those whose surroundings and possessions were primarily practical. The royal couple encouraged the development of electroplating and electroforming as well as 'Parian ware,' a type of porcelain made to imitate marble. They often allowed manufacturers to replicate items from the Royal Collection by these new methods.[58]

In her catalogue, *Passionate Patrons*, Leah Kharibian writes,

art played a key role in every aspect of their daily lives. As patrons and collectors their tastes were exceptionally wide-ranging, taking in all types of art from early Renaissance panel paintings to sculpture, furniture, jewellery, miniatures, watercolours and the new art of photography. As a couple they took a keen interest in the serious endeavors of cataloguing, conserving and displaying both their new acquisitions and the magnificent inheritance of the Royal Collection. But they enjoyed themselves immensely, too. A large proportion of their purchases were bought as gifts for each other—often as surprises. They took great delight in planning and participating in magnificent balls and fancy-dress parties, musical evenings and theatrical experiences.[59]

Victoria went to the theater or opera on thirty-six occasions during her coronation year alone, and she and Albert were patrons of both. They held many formal dances, including three costume balls. The most famous of these was a medieval-themed ball at Buckingham Palace in 1842 to benefit the silk weavers of Spitalfields. The royal couple received guests in the Throne Room, on a raised dais under an ornate gothic canopy, dressed as King Edward III and his consort

Queen Philippa of Hainault. Their splendid costumes were based on the real tomb effigies of their predecessors.

The design and decoration of the royal residences also engaged the Queen and Prince. They expanded Buckingham Palace, adding the east wing and the Renaissance-revival ballroom. In Scotland, they erected the current Balmoral Castle, which they decorated in a fanciful Scottish vernacular, with tartan and thistles. Prince Albert contributed to the design of Osborne House on the Isle of Wight. This included a sculpture gallery and served as an important showcase for the art that they collected.

The death of Prince Albert in 1861, at the age of forty-two, was a devastating tragedy for the Queen personally, and for the country. He was arguably the greatest public servant that Britain has ever had. Queen Victoria remained in mourning until her own death in 1901. She continued to advance the artistic genres and artists that he had championed, and that together they had cultivated, for the rest of her reign.

As the Pre-Raphaelites became part of a broader medieval revival the Brotherhood itself became somewhat redundant to their needs. The last public exhibition of their works as a group occurred in 1852. Two of Millais's pictures hung in the Royal Academy Exhibition that year: *A Huguenot* and *Ophelia*. The former depicts a young Protestant couple in France meeting in a garden during the St Bartholomew's Day massacre, when Roman Catholics murdered tens of the thousands of Calvinist Huguenots, over several weeks in 1572. The girl is pleading with her Protestant beau to wear the armband of a Roman Catholic to disguise himself so that he can escape the slaughter. While he holds her, gazing tenderly into her worried eyes, he gently removes the armband that she has tied around him, preferring martyrdom over even pretended apostasy. Millais had initially sketched this scene as a simple meeting of lovers in a brick-walled garden but on the advice of Holman Hunt he added the historic context, which he took from Mayerbeer's opera *Les Hugenots*.

The wonderful, meticulously rendered flowers and foliage in the garden are typical of the kind of botanical illustration that was immensely popular, particularly among watercolorists, in the Victorian era. The most famous of these was Marianne North whose skill at rendering flowers was honoured with the opening of a gallery in Kew Gardens permanently dedicated to her works in 1882. Millais's passion for setting his subject in rich, verdant, floral surroundings is nowhere more apparent than in his *Ophelia*.

Drawn from Shakespeare's *Hamlet*, the tragic story of Ophelia was ideally tailored to fit Victorian and specifically Pre-Raphaelite sensibility. Spurned by Prince Hamlet, she has fallen into a river, while picking flowers, and as she floats away, temporarily buoyed by the air trapped in her clothing, she sings. But as her clothes become saturated, the weight of the water pulls "the poor wretch from her melodious lay" down to a muddy death.[60] In his depiction of the scene, Millais painted flowers mentioned by Shakespeare floating downriver with Ophelia, but he added a red poppy as a symbol of sleep and death. Millais based his gorgeously overgrown riverbank on the Hogsmill River in Surrey where he painted for several hours a day, six days a week, for five months to capture the background. In the end he had to work inside a kind of duck blind to protect himself from the cold weather.

Millais finished the painting over the winter at his studio on Gower Street in London. He based the figure of Ophelia on the newly discovered model Elizabeth Siddal, who would go on to sit for, and later marry Dante Gabriel Rossetti. She would also become an artist in her own right. *Ophelia* remains one of the most recognizable of all the Pre-Raphaelite paintings. It hangs today in the Tate Britain in London and must be seen in person to be fully appreciated. Even the most detailed reproduction does not convey the awesome effect of glittering light captured by Millais, in particular where the lace of Ophelia's dress floats on the surface of the water.

Holman Hunt's painting for the 1852 exhibition was *The Hireling Shepherd*. Its subject was the neglect of duty, in this case by the titular shepherd, who ignores his flock to woo a pretty red-haired maid, showing her a death's head hawkmoth. Hunt meant to symbolize the retreat of churchmen into theological debate while their flocks were led astray for lack of moral guidance. The title is a reference to the biblical allegory of the Good Shepherd. Hunt achieved considerable success with this painting as it was awarded a prize when exhibited at Birmingham in 1853 and sold to a collector for 120 pounds. Hunt later observed that with Millais's picture of the Huguenots also winning a prize at an exhibition in Liverpool, "the double success of our School...[indicated that] the recognition of our claims was thus proved to be growing."[61]

After the amicable dissolution of the Pre-Raphaelite Brotherhood, the three artists who had been the primary force behind it, continued to discuss art with each other and to explore common aesthetics, but they pursued their careers separately. They began to inspire a number of other artists. These included Edward Burne-Jones, Arthur Hughes, William Morris, the photographer Julia Margaret Cameron, Frederick Leighton, Frank Dicksee, Frederick Sandys, Lawrence Alma-Tadema, Simeon Solomon, and John William Waterhouse, among others.

The Pre-Raphaelite conquest of the Victorian and Edwardian art world was eventually formalized with honors. Millais and Burne-Jones were given baronetcies; Leighton was given a barony; Holman Hunt received the Order of Merit as a personal gift from King Edward VII; Dicksee and Alma-Tadema were knighted.

In fact, there had long been affection for the Pre-Raphaelites at the palace. In the midst of the early controversy surrounding Millais's *Christ in the House of His Parents*, Queen Victoria had arranged for the painting to be shown privately for her at Windsor Castle. This was unprecedented. "I hope that it will not have any bad effects upon the Queen's mind," Millais joked nervously to Hunt.[62] Gordon Fleming in his biography of Millais suggests that it did not. The following year Prince Albert gave a speech to the Royal Academy in which he reminded the members of their obligation to encourage developing artists in terms unmistakably similar to Ruskin's defense of Millais.[63]

A more private, but in its own way equally momentous, embrace of the Pre-Raphaelites came earlier, in 1855. In January of that year, Millais and Charles Dickens met for the first time at a dinner party given by their mutual friend, Wilkie Collins. After dinner they had a long conversation. The following day, Dickens wrote Millais a letter, and sent it, along with an article from *Household Words*, about the London fire brigade, which was the subject of Millais's work-in-progress, *The Rescue*. The letter read:

> If you have in your mind any previous association with the pages in which [the article] appears (very likely you have none) it may be a rather disagreeable one. In that case I hope a word, frankly said, may make it pleasanter. Objecting very strongly to what I believed to be an unworthy use of your great powers, I once expressed the objection in this same journal. My opinion on that point is not in the least changed, but it has never dashed my admiration of your progress in what I suppose are higher and better things. In short, you

have given me such great reasons (in your works) to separate you from uncongenial association, that I wish to give you in return one little reason for doing the like by me.[64]

Millais accepted the olive branch. Thereafter they became true friends. When Dickens died in 1870 it was Millais who was summoned to his death bed to draw the final portrait of the great author.

CHAPTER TWO

THE MUSE

George Birbeck Hill recalled meeting Rossetti when the latter was painting the wall murals for the Oxford Union, between 1857 and 1859. This project, depicting scenes from Arthurian legend, was an important commission for Rossetti. His assistants were drawn from a slightly younger group of artists working in the Pre-Raphaelite style, including Hill's friends Edward Burne-Jones and William Morris, then recent graduates, as well as Valentine Cameron Prinsep and Arthur Hughes. The company entertained themselves in conversation on whatever topics caught their interest. Hill wrote that he "one day heard" Rossetti comment "that a beautiful young woman," at the time facing trial "on a charge of murdering her lover, ought not to be hanged, even if found guilty, as she was 'such a stunner'." When Hill "ventured to assert" that he "would have her hanged beautiful or ugly, there was a general outcry of the artistic set." One of the young painters exclaimed, "Oh Hill, you would never hang a stunner!"[1]

There was, perhaps, no higher compliment that could be paid by Rossetti, than to identify someone, in the parlance of his Victorian youth, as a "stunner." The word might be applied to anyone with the capacity to compel, or "stun," others into awed admiration. On several occasions Rossetti used the word to describe another artist whose talent he admired: he reported to his brother seeing "some mighty things by that real stunner, Leonardo," at the Louvre.[2] But there was one context in which the word was used most frequently and to greatest effect: in the description of feminine beauty. Emily J. Orlando defines "stunner" as "Rossetti's term for a woman so beautiful she ought to be painted."[3] It is a perfect definition.

The "stunner" was an essential element of Pre-Raphaelite painting from the very beginning. The artists searched for models who possessed the specific, though ineffable, qualities of aspect that would compliment the Pre-Raphaelite ideal. Fiona MacCarthy describes, "the Pre-Raphaelite sport of hunting 'stunners'."[4] If that sounds mercenary, perhaps it was. But it was also part of the process of realizing an intense artistic vision.

In contrast to the neoclassical symmetry and restrained emotion that characterized much of mid-Victorian portraiture, the Pre-Raphaelite woman was conceived as otherworldly, enigmatic, and richly expressive. She often appeared with unconventional features, voluminous hair—frequently red or auburn—arched brows, and full, sometimes parted lips. This vision favored sensuality and individuality over conventional prettiness; it celebrated a form of beauty that could appear melancholy, mystical, or commanding.

The Pre-Raphaelite woman served as the visual conduit for a variety of types. She might be depicted as muse, goddess, nymph, *femme fatale*, doomed lover, enchantress or sorceress, a sibylline or prophetic figure, a saint, or a literary heroine. Her beauty was often bound up with pathos, mystery, or danger—qualities that gave her a potent dramatic presence. At times passive and introspective, at others powerful and even domineering, the Pre-Raphaelite ideal embraced complexity over conformity. It was a beauty that invited interpretation and veneration, not merely admiration. As such, the feminine was saturated with meaning, central to the movement's distinctive blend of aestheticism, symbolism, and romantic intensity.

I. LIZZIE:

Elizabeth Siddal was the first of the "stunners." Her collaboration with the artists facilitated their breakthrough. In his memoir, *Pre-Raphaelitism and the Pre-Raphaelite Brotherhood*, William Holman Hunt recalled the evening, in 1849, when Walter Deverell, a friend and fellow painter, closely associated with the P.R.B. at its infancy, burst in upon Hunt and Rossetti during dinner, to tell them about his chance encounter with Miss Siddal.

"You fellows can't tell what a stupendously beautiful creature I have found," Deverell announced. "By Jove! she's like a queen," he said, "magnificently tall, with a lovely figure, a stately neck," and hair "like dazzling copper" that "shimmers with lustre as she waves it down." He waxed poetic over "the most delicate and finished modelling" of her face, which appeared "exactly like the carving of a Pheidean goddess." He asked them where they thought he had "lighted on this paragon of beauty?" It was a rhetorical question. Deverell explained that he had been out accompanying his mother on her rounds of shopping. They entered a milliner's showroom in Cranbourne Alley near Leicester Square. While the saleswoman was "tempting" his mother with the latest fashion in hats, Deverell, having nothing with which "to amuse" himself, "peered over the blind of a glass door at the back of the shop," which disclosed a workroom, "and there was this unexpected jewel." With his mother employed as an intermediary, for propriety's sake, Deverell made the acquaintance of Elizabeth Siddal, and engaged her to sit for him, representing the figure of Viola in his painting of *Twelfth Night, Act II, Scene IV.*[5]

Deverell would not have the opportunity to work with her again. Miss Siddal was immediately enlisted by the Pre-Raphaelites who competed with one another for her services as a model. Hunt painted her between 1849 and 1850 in *A Converted British Family Sheltering a Christian Missionary from the Persecution of the Druids* then again in *Valentine Rescuing Sylvia From Proteus.* Rossetti painted her for the first time in 1850, in watercolor over pen and ink, for what was likely an early version of, *"Hist!" Said Kate the Queen.* This illustration of Robert Browning's *Pippa Passes* was later completed on a separate canvas. The section of the original that featured Miss Siddal's image was cut out to make the portrait, *Rossovestita.* As in Deverell's *Twelfth Night,* both of Hunt's compositions depicted multiple figures. On the original canvas, so did Rossetti's.

It was John Everett Millais who first made use of Miss Siddal's full potential by isolating her image. In 1852, at the age of nineteen, she posed for Millais as Ophelia in his celebrated painting of the character's death from *Hamlet,* discussed in the previous chapter.

To achieve the realistic effect of Ophelia floating in the water, Miss Siddal posed for Millais under quite challenging conditions. Millais wanted authenticity in the scene, so he had a bathtub placed in his studio and filled with water. Miss

Siddal lay half-submerged in it for hours on end, wearing the antique silver dress that Millais had acquired for her costume. The process was arduous and uncomfortable. On one disastrous occasion, the lamps that Millais had set up under the bathtub, to warm the water, burned out, with the artist too absorbed in his work to notice, and the model too professional to break pose, even as the water gradually cooled to a chill. Miss Siddal emerged with what was probably a case of pneumonia. Her father insisted that Millais pay for her medical care.

The relationship between Elizabeth Siddal and Dante Gabriel Rossetti proved to be different than the others. Lizzie—as he knew her—became Rossetti's muse. As Stephanie Chatfield writes in *The Pre-Raphaelite Sisterhood*, "Lizzie sat exclusively for Gabriel and he drew and painted her image obsessively. Again and again, he captured her likeness."[6] Their relationship deepened beyond artist and model, developing into a passionate love affair, that led to their engagement in 1854. However, Rossetti's unconventional lifestyle and Lizzie's fragile health delayed their marriage until 1860.

Lizzie showed a talent for painting and drawing. Rossetti encouraged her to pursue her own art. He became a mentor, providing practical instruction and guidance. Part of her success as a model had been a natural sympathy for the ideas of the Pre-Raphaelite Brotherhood. According to John Guille Millais, the artist's son and biographer, Lizzie "had read Tennyson" from an early age, "having first come to know something about him by finding one or two of his poems on a piece of paper which she brought home to her mother wrapped around a pat of butter."[7] She instinctually understood the influences that had contributed to Pre-Raphaelitism. Lizzie began to produce highly innovative watercolors and chalk drawings, clearly inspired by Rossetti's style and the themes of Tennyson's Arthurian revival, but distinctly her own. She was the only female artist whose work was shown at the Pre-Raphaelite group exhibition at No. 4 Russell Place, Fitzroy Square, London, in 1857.

The marriage was strained, in the end, amid rumors of her drug addiction and his neglect, or infidelity. Whether one problem caused the other, or vice versa, or whether there was much truth to either rumor, must remain the secrets of the dead. What is certain is that Lizzie was suffering from emotional and physical stress, compounded by grief, after the stillbirth of their child, when she died at the age of thirty two.

Ford Madox Brown recorded an interesting item in his diary for 10 March 1855, during the long period of engagement, between Rossetti and Siddal. He had received a letter from Rossetti, informing him that John Ruskin had bought all of Lizzie's drawings, "and said they beat Rossetti's own." Brown wrote, "This is like Ruskin, the incarnation of exaggeration. However, he is right to admire them. She is a stunner and no mistake. Rossetti once told me that, when he first saw her, he felt his destiny was defined. Why does he not marry her?"[8] It is noteworthy that Brown seems to employ the word "stunner" here in the broadest sense, encompassing both her beauty and her talent.

Given the prominence of sensuality, and implications of sexuality, in the paintings of the Pre-Raphaelite Brotherhood, it was perhaps inevitable that the love lives of the artists would come to define their public images. Their romances were often sensational. One relationship in particular necessitated a split between one of the artists and his greatest patron.

II. EFFIE:

John Ruskin believed that "wise work" has three characteristics: it is honest, it is useful, and it is cheerful.

Ruskin looked with admiration upon the gothic architecture of the Middle Ages. He determined, writes P.D. Anthony, in *John Ruskin's Labour*, "that it required forms of social organization and forms of manual labour that are superior to those of contemporary society" and "which are essential to human development and happiness." Modest masons and craftsmen working in their own limited spheres had the opportunity "to express themselves in magnificent creations which transcended the humble contributions of ordinary men."[9]

By the 1850s Ruskin was contemplating "a great work" he meant "to write on politics—founded on the thirteenth century." However Nicholas Shrimpton writes, in *The Cambridge Companion to John Ruskin*, that by the end of the decade he "had turned away from overt medievalism to a deeper, more implicit use of medieval assumptions. Pre-modern concepts, such as intrinsic value and the 'just price,' were applied to modern problems in a series of controversial books and lectures."[10]

In the 1870s Ruskin founded the Guild of St George. Its mission was to encourage arts education, independent craftsmanship, and sustainable agriculture among the working classes. He attempted to spread the message of the guild through a series of pamphlets collectively titled, *Fors Clavigera*. Shrimpton writes, "these texts would seek to suggest an alternative to the industrialism, capitalism, and urbanization of modern society."[11]

Ruskin's program was the inspiration for the Arts and Crafts movement developed by William Morris in the 1880s. Morris's philosophy was a somewhat uneasy amalgamation of Ruskinian and Marxist ideas. But Ruskin's own critique of *laissez-faire* came from another direction. Anthony cites a "political analysis characterized by Carlyle in 1838 as 'Götzism', after Goethe."[12] Shrimpton insists that he was not "an ancestor of the British Labour Party" and that "[n]either the Marxian nor the Fabian branch of English socialism was significantly Ruskinian."[13] He had been raised a strict Calvinist, and although he had a religious crisis in middle age, Anthony writes, his "Christian faith developed and broadened as he grew older."[14]

Ruskin was just beginning his transition from art critic to social critic when he married Euphemia Chalmers Gray, called "Effie," in the drawing room of her parents' house in the Highlands of Scotland, in April of 1848. The marriage was a disaster. It would end in one of the great scandals of the Victorian period, inviting widespread speculation about Ruskin's sexual persuasion. Not incidentally, the Pre-Raphaelites were at the center of the scandal.

Effie Gray had met John Ruskin for the first time when she was twelve. He was ten years older. Their families had long been acquainted. Effie would stay with the Ruskins when traveling to and from her boarding school in Stratford upon Avon, and they provided a safe haven for her, when she and her younger sisters fell ill with scarlet fever. At the age of nineteen, Effie visited London and rekindled her friendship with Ruskin. By then he had published the first volumes of *Modern Painters*.

The newlyweds spent their wedding night at a nearby inn in Perthshire. The marriage was not consummated. Nor would it ever be over the subsequent six years of their marriage. Ruskin consistently refused to have sexual intercourse with his wife, leaving her in a position of miserable neglect. Effie would later write to her father:

> He alleged various reasons, hatred to children, religious motives, a desire to preserve my beauty, and, finally this last year he told me his true reason...that he had imagined women were quite different to what he saw I was, and that

the reason he did not make me his Wife was because he was disgusted with my person the first evening 10th April.[15]

Ruskin himself corroborated these words during the eventual annulment of their marriage. He commented that, though Effie was beautiful, "her person was not formed to excite passion. On the contrary, there were certain circumstances in her person which completely checked it."[16] What were these circumstances? The most persistent rumor over the intervening century and a half is that Ruskin was horrified by his first encounter with female genitalia. As a virgin who had only ever seen nude women in alabaster statuary and modest paintings, he was in some way unprepared for, and unwilling to accept, the natural female form. There was certainly nothing *unnatural* about Effie's body: her subsequent happy marriage to John Everett Millais produced eight children.

The Ruskins had been married for three years when John Ruskin penned his decisive apology for the Pre-Raphaelites in the London *Times*. He subsequently took an active interest in their careers. In this context it was natural that Millais made the acquaintance of Effie Ruskin. After all, it was Millais specifically whom Ruskin had been defending in his open letter, and Millais who stood out to Ruskin as the most promising member of the Pre-Raphaelite Brotherhood.

Effie sat for Millais for the first time in 1852, probably at her husband's suggestion. Millais's painting, *The Order of Release*, depicted a Scottish highlander being discharged from prison into the custody of his family. Effie modeled for the character of the wife. The painting was a tremendous success for Millais. When it was exhibited at the Royal Academy in 1853, *The Illustrated London News* reported that the young artist had, "a larger crowd of admirers in his little corner...than all the Academicians put together."[17]

Beginning in July of 1853, the Ruskins and Millais spent the summer together in a rented cottage near Glenfinlas in the Scottish Highlands. Ruskin had commissioned Millais to paint him against a background of "a lovely piece of worn rock, with foaming water, and weeds, and moss, and a noble overhanging bank of dark crag," as Ruskin described the scene in a letter to his father.[18] It had the potential to be, in the words of Suzanne Fagence Cooper, "the archetypal Pre-Raphaelite picture, a detailed study of natural forms combined with a portrait of the art movement's most vocal supporter."[19] The result was indeed one of the finest portraits ever painted of Ruskin, though it would always have bitter associations for the man himself.

During that summer Millais and Effie grew to be close friends. They were often left alone together by Ruskin. The development of romantic feelings between the artist and his patron's wife can be seen in the increasingly tender sketches that he drew of her. Cooper writes, in her book, *Effie*, "He painted her sitting beside a waterfall, or quietly sewing, with foxgloves tucked into her hair."[20] They shared innocent, but indiscreet, moments of intimacy, like waiting out a rainstorm together beneath a shawl. Meanwhile Millais was confronted with the reality of the Ruskins' marriage. In the little cottage Ruskin slept on the sofa, not with his wife, and he displayed little affection for her. By the time Millais returned to London, Cooper continues, he had begun to fear that Ruskin "deliberately left him alone with Effie to force her into a compromising position."[21] Effie shared this suspicion. Was Ruskin trying to extricate himself from a marriage that he did not want to prolong, in a way that would shift guilt to his wife, and acquit him of blame? If this was Ruskin's gambit, he achieved a pyrrhic victory.

Effie and Millais did fall in love. She proceeded to end her marriage to Ruskin. In the course of the annulment, she submitted herself to a physical examination that would refute any claims of infidelity on her part, by establishing her virginity. The examining physicians, including Queen Victoria's obstetrician, Dr. Charles Locock, certified that she was indeed *virgo intacta.* The marriage was legally annulled on grounds that, "the said John Ruskin was incapable of consummating the same by reason of incurable impotency."[22]

John Everett Millais and Euphemia Gray were married in July of 1855. She waited seven months from the time of the annulment of her first marriage to see Millais again, "partly to heal her nerves," Rachel Cambell-Johnson writes in *The Times*, "partly to test Millais's commitment."[23] There was surely never any doubt of his affection. They remained devoted to each other for the remainder of their lives.

The artist's son, John Guille Millais, wrote of his parents' marriage:

And here let me say at once how much of my father's happiness in after years was due to the chief event of this [his wedding] day. During the forty-one years of their married life my mother took the keenest interest in his work, and did all in her power to contribute to his success, taking upon herself not only the care of the household and the management of family affairs, but the great bulk of his correspondence, and saving him an infinity of trouble by personally ascertaining the objects of his callers (an ever increasing multitude) before admitting them into his presence...Possessed in a considerable degree of the artistic sense, she was happily free from the artistic temperament, whilst her knowledge of history proved also a valuable acquisition. When an historical picture was in contemplation, she delighted to study anew the circumstances and the characters to be depicted, and to gather for her husband's use all particulars as to the scene and the costumes of the period.[24]

Millais grew rich and respectable over those four decades, culminating in his elevation to a baronetcy in 1885. During her youth the author Beatrix Potter knew Sir John as a family friend. Her father Rupert Potter was a member of Millais's social circle. His photographs of Millais at home in his London studio at 2 Palace Gate, Kensington, depict a setting that looks more like a minor palace or a club in St. James's than an artist's studio. The painting *Lilacs* and a portrait of the 5th Earl of Rosebery, which appear on easels in a photograph, dated July of 1886, are the only indication of the gentleman's profession.

Beatrix Potter was herself an accomplished illustrator, principally of her own *Peter Rabbit* stories. She was a prolific watercolorist whose landscapes and studies of mushrooms, animals, plants, and insects were displayed at the Victoria and Albert in 2022, in the exhibition, *Drawn to Nature*.

On his death in August of 1896, Potter wrote in her journal that she would "always have a most affectionate remembrance" of Millais, though she was "unmercifully afraid of him as a child" on account of his teasing "schoolboy manner." Despite this fact she was not afraid to show him her drawings. He gave her "the kindest encouragement" and complimented her, saying, "plenty of people can draw, but you and my son John have observation." She concluded, "He was an honest fine man."[25]

Any hint of scandal that attended the marriage of John and Effie Millais faded over time. Queen Victoria, who had received Effie at court as Mrs. Ruskin, was bound by palace protocols to keep her at a distance as Mrs. Millais, even as Lady Millais. The annulment had introduced topics of scandal that could only embarrass the Queen by association. However, shortly before

Millais's death, the Queen received Effie for a private audience, signaling that the marriage had royal approval after all. It was a final gesture of good will to an artist whom Her Majesty had quietly supported since her private viewing of *Christ in the House of His Parents*.

According to Cooper's analysis, "Effie became the heroine of a great Victorian love story. Her life reads like a novel, full of color, sensation, despair, and romance. Her first husband was a damaged genius, her second a handsome rebel."[26] Certainly, a sense of the injustice done to her, combined with her and Millais's patient love and exemplary marriage, made Effie the sympathetic figure in the drama.

III: FANNY AND EDITH:

William Holman Hunt's marriage to Fanny Waugh in 1865 seemed to herald a period of personal happiness for the artist. Fanny was the daughter of a London chemist. Hunt had begun courting her after a failed engagement to his model Annie Miller. It is likely that Fanny would have become an important model for the artist and his circle. The Pre-Raphaelite sculptor Thomas Woolner described her as, "one of the grandest creatures I ever saw and her face is not far from what I want for my Lady: I hope to get her to sit."[27] The union, however, was short-lived. Fanny fell gravely ill, and in 1866, while the couple was in Italy, she died of complications from childbirth. The loss deeply affected Hunt, who depicted her in the painting, *Isabella and the Pot of Basil*, as a figure of grief and mourning.

The Reverend Robert Loftus Tottenham, chaplain of Holy Trinity Anglican Church in Florence presided over the funeral of Hunt's wife and the christening of his son less than a week apart in December of 1866. Hunt named the newborn boy Cyril Benoni, the middle name meaning "son of sorrow" in Hebrew.

Hunt took up residence in one of the old Medici villas near Fiesole, converting the stables into a studio. There he carved his wife's tomb, which was placed on her grave in the English Cemetery in Florence near that of Elizabeth Barrett Browning. Hunt donated a silver chalice to Holy Trinity in his wife's memory, inscribed with her name. In 1938 his daughter Gladys donated a matching silver paten in memory of Fanny's son, her half-brother, Cyril, who had by then died, at the age of sixty-seven. It was inscribed, "In dear and grateful remembrance of Cyril Benoni Holman Hunt born in Florence Oct 27 1866 died in Bridport 25 July 1934."[28] Both pieces can be seen today at Saint Mark's English Church in Florence, the present Anglican parish of that city.

On their return to England, Fanny's youngest sister, Edith, became the boy's guardian. Hunt found solace with his former sister-in-law. Edith professed her love for Hunt while he painted her in a portrait commonly called, *The Birthday*, as her father had commissioned it on the occasion of her twenty first. Their relationship, however, faced significant obstacles. According to the English marriage laws of the time, a man was prohibited from marrying his deceased wife's sister. This legal constraint meant that Hunt and Edith could not marry in England, which led to their prolonged engagement, during which time Hunt traveled alone in the Holy Land.

Hunt had been visiting Syria, Egypt, and Palestine regularly since the 1850s to gather ethnographic details for his biblical paintings. In the course of his sojourn to Jerusalem in 1869 he began work on a portrait of Jesus, entitled, *The Shadow of Death*, which he finished in 1874. The painting depicts the young Christ in his carpentry shop in Nazareth, stretching his arms after a day's work. The light of the setting sun casts his shadow on a wooden tool-rack, forming a cruciform shape, foreshadowing as it were, his death on the cross. Hunt's treatment emphasized the connection between Christ's humble work as a carpenter and his great work as the Savior of mankind.

The separation from Edith was undoubtedly challenging for both, but it also demonstrated their commitment to one another. The relationship was seen by many as transgressive. The Waugh family objected. Thomas Woolner, whose suit of marriage had been rejected by Fanny, and who later married a third sister, Alice, supported their objections. This led to a severing of ties between various Pre-Raphaelite Brothers. "Gabriel of late years hated him," wrote William Michael Rossetti, of Woolner.[29] The eventual decision by Hunt and Edith to marry abroad underscores their determination to be together despite these constraints. In 1875, they traveled to Neuchâtel in Switzerland, where they were legally married.

Hunt's family life was complex. His first marriage to Fanny had produced a son, Cyril. His second marriage to Edith produced two children: a daughter, Gladys, and a son, Hilary. Despite the unconventional nature of this arrangement—the children were cousins as well as siblings—the Hunts enjoyed a stable and loving family life, which revolved naturally around the practice of art.

Edith proved to be a supportive partner, managing the household and assisting Hunt with his work. The couple's life together was characterized by respect and dedication. Hunt's later works, often imbued with themes of redemption and resurrection, may have been influenced by his experiences of loss and love within his family.

IV. JANE MORRIS:

Unlike Millais and Hunt, who emerged from the turmoil of their public love triangles with reputations intact, Dante

Gabriel Rossetti was never quite able to escape from the public judgement of his private life. Like Lord Byron his celebrity was both helped and hindered by the perception that he was a brooding decadent, perhaps a rake or *roué*.

In 2017 the Morgan Library in New York opened an exhibition on the life and work of the author Henry James. This was the sort of show that the Morgan does best: manuscripts, early editions, letters, portraits, along with paintings by contemporary artists. It was titled, *Henry James and American Painting*. One item in particular caught the attention of anyone interested in the Pre-Raphaelites. It was a letter that James wrote to his friend, the artist John La Farge. In it he describes a visit to Rossetti's studio.

Bostonian by birth, Henry James came to England in early 1869. He would remain there for the rest of his life, being naturalized as a British subject in 1915. He was introduced to Rossetti a few months after his arrival in London by their mutual friend Charles Norton. James admired the Pre-Raphaelites and had already visited the studios of several related artists. He assessed Rossetti's work in perceptive but also candid and amusing terms in the letter to La Farge, dated June of 1869. It read:

I did see Rossetti, Chas. Norton having conducted me to his studio—in the most delicious melancholy old house at Chelsea on the river. When I think what Englishmen ought to be, with such homes & haunts! Rossetti however, does not shame his advantages. Personally, he struck me as unattractive—poor man, I suppose he was horribly bored!—but his pictures, as I saw them in his room, I think decidedly strong. They were all large fanciful portraits of women, of the type *que vous savez*, narrow, special, monotonous, but with lots of beauty & power. His chief inspiration & constant model is

Mrs. Wm. Morris, whom I had seen, a woman of extraordinary beauty of a certain sort—a face, in fact quite made to his hand. He has painted a dozen portraits of her—one, in particular, in a blue gown, with her hair down, pressing a lot of lilies against her breast—an almost great work.[30]

Rossetti's "most delicious melancholy old house" was located at 16 Cheyne Walk where it still stands today. An 1882 watercolor by Henry Treffry Dunn gives us a glimpse of the interior at the time: sea-green walls and upholstery; piles of lush Persian rugs; Delft tiles around the fireplace; paintings, mirrors, and religious images in gilt frames on the walls. At this point Rossetti was at the height of his talents. He would spend the next decade painting what were arguably the definitive expressions of the Pre-Raphaelite style: lush, detailed, accomplished works.

The crisis of Rossetti's career—his passionate but ill-fated marriage to Elizabeth Siddal—was over. The ending had been most tragic. On a February evening in 1862 he returned home to find his wife comatose from an overdose of laudanum. Though Rossetti called several physicians, they could do nothing, and she died the next morning. It may have been a deliberate suicide. William Bell Scott wrote that she had "pinned a written statement on the breast of her night-shirt and put an end to her troubles, real or imaginary."[31] The note was supposedly taken off her by Rossetti and destroyed by Ford Madox Brown. None of that can be proved.

Rossetti buried Lizzie with the manuscripts of his unpublished poetry in her coffin. This romantic gesture came to a ghoulish end, however. He later ordered her body exhumed to retrieve the poems. Afterward, he wrote to the poet Algernon Charles Swinburne:

I want to tell you something lest you should hear it first from any one else. It is that I have recovered my old book of poems. Friends had long hinted such a possibility to me but it was only just lately I made up my mind to it. I hope you will think none the worse of my feeling for the memory of one for whom I know you had a true regard. The truth is, that no one so much as herself would have approved of my doing this... Art was the only thing which she felt very seriously. Had it been possible to her, I should have found the book on my pillow the night she was buried; and could she have opened the grave, no other hand would have been needed.[32]

Lizzie had influenced the aesthetic of the "Pre-Raphaelite Woman" with her red hair and pale skin. William Rossetti characterized her as "a most beautiful creature with an air between dignity and sweetness." He described her as "tall, finely formed with a lofty neck and regular yet somewhat uncommon features." She had "greenish-blue unsparkling eyes, brilliant complexion and a lavish heavy wealth of copper-golden hair."[33] Georgiana Burne-Jones, the wife of artist Edward Burne-Jones, wrote of Siddal's "beautiful deep-red hair," and her complexion, which looked "as if a rose tint lay beneath the white skin, producing a most soft and delicate pink."[34]

Rossetti's most famous painting of her was done from memory and sketch studies after her death. *Beata Beatrix* represents Beatrice Portinari, the subject of Dante Alighieri's courtly love poem, *La Vita Nuova*. Lizzie-as-Beatrice is portrayed transfigured in prayer at the moment before her death. The painting connects Rossetti's own love for Lizzie with his namesake's grieving love for the doomed Beatrice. It is a subject rich in spiritual connotations. Beatrice reappears in the *Divine Comedy* as Dante's guide into Paradise.

For all that influence, one tends to agree with Henry James that it was Jane Morris—and, moreover, Alexa Wilding—who were Rossetti's indispensable muses. At the very least they complimented a more mature talent than Rossetti possessed during Lizzie's lifetime. James had met Jane Morris several months earlier in the company of her husband, the artist William Morris. James described her in positively glowing terms in a letter to his sister Alice dated March of 1869:

> *Je n'en reviens pas*—she haunts me still. A figure cut out of a missal—out of one of Rossetti's or Hunt's pictures—to say this gives but a faint idea of her, because when such an image puts on flesh and blood, it is an apparition of fearful and wonderful intensity. It's hard to say [whether] she's a grand synthesis of all the pre-Raphaelite pictures ever made—or they a 'keen analysis' of her—whether she's an original or a copy. In either case she is a wonder. Imagine a tall lean woman in a long dress of some dead purple stuff, guiltless of hoops (or of anything else, I should say) with a mass of crisp black hair heaped into great wavy projections on each of her temples, a thin pale face, a pair of strange, sad, deep, dark Swinburnish eyes, with great thick black oblique brows, joined in the middle and tucking themselves under her hair, a mouth like 'Oriana' in our illustrated Tennyson, a long neck, without any collar, and in lieu thereof some dozen strings of outlandish beads—in fine Complete. On the wall was a large nearly full-length portrait of her by Rossetti, so strange and unreal that if you hadn't seen her, you'd pronounce it a distempered vision, but in fact an extremely good likeness.[35]

James seemed to sense the sexual magnetism between artist and model. By all accounts Rossetti and Jane Morris carried on a long affair during her marriage to the painfully un-sexual Morris. This was made all the more awkward by the fact that Rossetti lived with the Morrises for months at a time at Kelmscott Manor in Oxfordshire where he and William were artistic collaborators. Whether out of misguided hero-worship for Rossetti, or some perverse tenet of socialism (Morris wrote a utopian novel that imagined a world without marriage), Morris suffered to live with this arrangement. And he must have known that he was the butt of ridicule for it.

At his house in Cheyne Walk, Rossetti kept a menagerie of exotic animals. This included peacocks, owls, parakeets, armadillos, kangaroos, a Brahmin bull, donkeys, and a raccoon who lived in a chest of drawers.

Most of the animals were purchased through Charles Jamrach, a dealer of wild animals with premises in Ratcliffe Highway. Jamrach was well known, mentioned by name in *Dracula* by Bram Stoker: a wolf that escapes from the Zoological Gardens in Regent's Park is "one of three grey ones that came from Norway to Jamrach's, which we bought off him four years ago."[36]

In September of 1869, Rossetti acquired the jewel of his collection: a wombat. His interest in the marsupials had evidently been cultivated at the same Regent's Park Zoo, where several were exhibited. In a letter to Ford Madox Brown in July of 1860, he wrote, "Dear Brown: Lizzie [Siddal] and I propose to meet Georgie and Ned [Burne-Jones] at 2 pm tomorrow at the Zoological Gardens—place of meeting, the Wombat's Lair."[37] An early appearance of a wombat in Rossetti's art can be seen in the frontispiece illustration he made for his sister Christina's book, *Goblin Market*, in 1865.

The wombat that Rossetti purchased from Jamrach was short lived, as were many of his rather irresponsibly housed pets. Rossetti named the creature "Top," in what seems to have been a reference to the plump, hirsute William Morris, whom

Rossetti was cuckolding. Morris had long been known to friends by the nickname "Topsy." A sketch by Rossetti of Jane Morris leading the wombat Top by a leash can be seen to underscore the point.

The wombat died on November 6, 1869. Rossetti commemorated the event with a sketch of himself in mourning. Angus Trumble writes, in *The Public Domain Review*, that the portrait "is satirical but was apparently prompted by genuine grief."[38] Rossetti wrote a stanza of verse to accompany it:

> I never reared a young wombat
>> To glad me with his pin-hole eye,
>> But when he most was sweet and fat
>> And tailless, he was sure to die![39]

To his credit William Morris seems finally to have stood up for himself. In July of 1874 Rossetti left Kelmscott suddenly, never to return.

V: THE WATERHOUSE MUSE:

Repeated collaborations between an artist and a model were common in the Pre-Raphaelite movement. John William Waterhouse was among the last painters to make use of the Pre-Raphaelite style in direct continuity with the first generation of Pre-Raphaelite painters. He was not strictly a Pre-Raphaelite. His interest in classical and mythological subjects placed him, with Sir Lawrence Alma-Tadema, somewhat out of the mainstream of the genre. However a series of Arthurian, Shakespearian, and Christian paintings in the 1890s are boldly Pre-Raphaelite in style.

Beginning in the 1890s, and continuing until his death in 1917, Waterhouse worked primarily with one female model.

Her likeness appears in his most famous works: *La Belle Dame sans Merci* (1893); *A Naiad, or Hylas with a Nymph* (1893); *Ophelia* (1894); *The Mermaid* (1901); and *Tristan and Isolde* (1914). In one of his most famous paintings, *Hylas and the Nymphs* (1896), she appears duplicated as multiple figures.

For many years there was a mystery surrounding the identity of this model. "Who was she?" Christopher Wood asked in his 1981 book, *The Pre-Raphaelites*. "One cannot help speculating about the identity of the mysterious and beautiful model who reappears so often in...Waterhouse's pictures...It remains one of the few Pre-Raphaelite mysteries, and one that will probably never be solved."[40]

The "Waterhouse Girl," as she was long known, is a striking and prepossessing beauty. Her looks are characterized by up-turned eyes, celestial nose, a modest sensuality about the lips, and the long reddish-golden hair associated with Pre-Raphaelite models since Rossetti's early paintings of Elizabeth Siddal. Peter Trippi writes that, "given their three decade relationship," she "surely functioned as the artist's muse."[41] We see her age over time from a young seductress in the earliest works to a woman of dignity and adult beauty in later paintings such as *The Soul of the Rose, or My Sweet Rose* (1908) and *The Annunciation* (1914). That Waterhouse changed his themes and approach to suit his model, rather than the other way around, is a tribute to her profound influence on his work.

The mystery of the model's identity was at last solved. In 1988 a pencil study by Waterhouse for his 1905 painting *Lamia* was bequeathed to the Yale Center for British Art in New Haven, Connecticut. It depicts the upturned face of the model. Her name is inscribed by Waterhouse on the paper: Miss Muriel Foster.[42]

We are fortunate to know her name, not as a mere piece of trivia. Waterhouse's best work had for its foundation one of the most successful partnerships between artist and model in the history of painting. Muriel Foster's contribution to that partnership comes through to viewers today. As Rossetti wrote in another context, "Beauty like hers is genius."[43] Perhaps this genius is the secret of the Pre-Raphaelite "stunners."

CHAPTER THREE

SECRET GARDEN

The Victorians inherited from the Georgians a glorious tradition of landscape gardening, both in the neoclassical and the more naturalistic Romantic styles. The landscape gardens of the eighteenth century had been projects of the nobility, located on the great country estates. These projects were of course ongoing in the nineteenth century, but the Victorian period witnessed a blossoming of horticulture in the commons, characterized by the proliferation of public gardens and small-scale formal gardens in middle-class homes.

According to historians at English Heritage, "An extraordinary number of innovations in the study, cultivation and display of plants were made during the Victorian period. At the same time there was an explosion of interest in gardening, which became a national obsession." Most notably, "Advances in the way plants were transported and transplanted meant that botanists were able to raise specimens imported from all over the world."[1]

Early Victorian gardens were characterized by formalism

and artifice. The influential garden designer, botanist, and writer John Claudius Loudon led fashion away from the Romantic style which had accentuated and imitated nature. Loudon believed that garden design should be asserted as an art with bold use of exotic plants and geometric design. He popularized the term "landscape architecture."

Loudon was an advocate of public gardens and greenbelts. Like his American counterpart, Frederick Law Olmsted, later in the century, he believed that parks should be incorporated into cities through urban planning. Loudon designed what is often described as Britain's first public park, the Derby Arboretum. According to historians at English Heritage, "Urban parks" were "created in response to concern about overcrowding and the condition of the poor." These public gardens were similar to their private counterparts in "layout and planting, but with amenities such as bandstands and tea houses."[2] Loudon coined the word arboretum for a botanic garden in which trees, both indigenous and exotic, were cultivated and studied.

The systematic cultivation of plants became a serious endeavor throughout the British Empire in the nineteenth century. Botanic gardens were established in colonies throughout the world to meet agricultural, medicinal, and economic needs. The earliest of these had been established in the eighteenth century. Jim Endersby writes, in *The Financial Times*, that:

St Vincent, in the West Indies, was the first colony to found such a garden (in 1765), and Britain's East India Company decided it would be profitable to found one at Calcutta soon after (1787).

Eventually, there would be a network of gardens that spanned the globe, which would prove vital to the British Empire, allowing...crops like rubber and cinchona (the tree from whose bark quinine was extracted) to be collected outside the empire and moved to colonies where they could be grown profitably. (Think about all those rubber trees that now form forests in southeast Asia; their scientific name is Hevea brasiliensis, meaning "from Brazil".)[3]

Back in England around the same time the royal pleasure gardens at Kew were being transformed into a center for scientific cultivation under King George III. The monarch appointed his horticultural advisor Sir Joseph Banks to the directorship of Kew Gardens in 1797. Banks envisioned Kew as the "great botanical exchange house for the empire." To that end he coordinated ambitious programs of exchange between the many fledgling botanic gardens throughout the colonies.

By the time Queen Victoria ascended the throne, Kew Gardens had fallen on hard times. After her grandfather's stewardship, they had been neglected. The government was considering a plan to close Kew in order to save money. Endersby writes:

In 1838, the botanist John Lindley was asked to report on the plan, but instead of closure, he proposed the government should remove the garden from royal control and run it directly. His rationale was that there were already "many gardens in British Colonies and dependencies...in Calcutta, Bombay, Sahranpur...at Sydney, and in Trinidad, costing many thousands a year". Yet, the value of these gardens "is very much diminished by the want of some system under which they can all be regulated and controlled". Yet if proper co-ordination could be established, the empire's gardens were "capable of conferring very important benefits upon commerce and...colonial prosperity."[4]

The government accepted Lindsey's recommendations and in 1840 Kew was adopted as a national botanic garden. Under this arrangement it flourished as the "great botanical exchange house for the empire" first proposed by Banks. The scale and efficiency with which exotic plants were imported during the nineteenth century made them available to individual home gardeners as well as professionals.

The style and philosophy of landscape gardening changed subtly at the end of the century. The gardens of the Late-Victorian period emphasized the vernacular and domestic. Designers eschewed the extreme artifice of both the classical and faux-natural Romantic styles in favor of the homely, practical, and lovely. "Let there be some formalism about the house to carry on the geometric lines and enclosed feeling of architecture," advised Henry Avray Tipping, the architectural editor of *Country Life* magazine, "but let us step shortly from that into wood and wild garden."[5] Tippering was speaking in 1928 but he was describing an ideal that had been established in the Late-Victorian and Edwardian periods. The primary influence was the Arts and Crafts movement, associated with William Morris, and inspired by the aesthetics of the Pre-Raphaelite Movement.

Helena Gerrish in *The English Garden* writes, "Beyond the formal 'outside rooms' that were viewed from the house, the Arts & Crafts garden gave way to the landscape, with rock gardens leading to woodland glades, and wild areas with rustic paths and water gardens."[6] According to historians at English Heritage, "The interest in vernacular architecture encouraged by the Arts and Crafts movement led designers to imitate cottage gardens by reviving long-neglected plants...It embodied the respect for the past which the Victorians maintained, even at their most innovative and experimental."[7]

I. OVER THE GARDEN WALL:

The conception of the garden as a space that is both interior and exterior finds expression in the walled gardens that provide a common setting in Pre-Raphaelite art and poetry. Use of this setting by William Morris, in his 1858 poem, *The Defence of Guenevere*,[8] and Christina Rossetti, in her 1862 poem, "Shut Out,"[9] are representative of a whole range of others. The Pre-Raphaelites drew upon biblical, medieval, and Renaissance symbolism related to the walled garden. But they reinterpreted those symbols to represent the inner and outer realms of personal experience.

Writing in the journal, *Victorian Poetry*, Dinah Roe argues that, "the Pre-Raphaelite revival of the enclosed garden modernizes what was once a medieval space by remaking the traditional *hortus conclusus* in the image of the nineteenth-century artistic mind." For Morris and Christina Rossetti, "the enclosed garden's paradoxical nature (open / closed; natural / artificial; free / constrained)" informed a "portrayal of consciousness as fluid, multivalent and self-generating" in the Pre-Raphaelite genre.[10]

The first enclosed garden was Eden, the paradise created by God for Adam and Eve, from which the first man and the first woman were later expelled, for eating of the fruit of the Tree of the Knowledge of Good and Evil. The garden's boundaries, which had enclosed the world of Adam and Eve, became inverted at the Fall. The inner paradise of Eden became an unreachable outer realm, where God placed Cherubim and a flaming sword to block the entrance and prevent mankind from partaking prematurely of the Tree of Life.

The phrase *hortus conclusus*, which means, literally, "garden enclosed," comes from the Latin translation of the Bible. Song of Solomon 4:12 reads: "A garden enclosed is my sister, my spouse; a spring shut up, a fountain sealed." This verse is part of a larger poetic exchange between lovers and uses the imagery of a garden to describe the beloved's purity, beauty, and exclusivity. The "fountain sealed" indicates a source of life and sustenance that is kept pure and inaccessible to all but the rightful lover.

During the Middle Ages, this passage from Song of Solomon was interpreted in two ways. Broadly, it was taken to foreshadow the mystical marriage between Jesus Christ and his Church. The Church was understood as the Bride of Christ, and the enclosed garden a metaphor of the Church as a people set apart. The passage was also interpreted in reference to Mary, the mother of Jesus. The protected or secluded garden was a reference to Mary's virginity at the time when God made her pregnant. She was the "fountain sealed up" in that context. The walled garden was a pattern of her body, the vessel through which Christ, and all mankind's hope for Eden restored, would grow into the world. Renaissance artwork often depicted Mary within or beside an enclosed garden. This is seen in Fra Angelico's *Annunciation* of 1430 and in the 1510 *Virgin and Child* of Gerard David, the Early Netherlandish painter. Dante Gabriel Rossetti revived the same tradition, in his 1849 painting, *The Girlhood of Mary Virgin*. Rossetti depicted the trellis of the garden being actually constructed around her.

In the poems of Morris and Christina Rossetti, the walled garden is presented as a metaphor of the inner self. Morris's poem allows Guenevere to "encounter her erotic self" in the *hortus conclusus*, as Roe put it.[11] Rossetti uses a locked garden that the narrator cannot enter as a metaphor for alienation.

The meanings attributed by Pre-Raphaelite artists to the garden can be read by extension into the plants themselves.

II. THE LANGUAGE OF FLOWERS:

Floriography is a system of symbolism attached to the various species of flowers, allowing for the communication of emotions or ideas, through the selection and arrangement of blossoms. This unique mode of expression reached its zenith in Britain in the nineteenth century, when enthusiasm for gardening was taken up in earnest by the middle classes, and household gardens became ubiquitous. The subtleties of meaning conveyed in floral arrangements provided a discreet means for people to convey unspoken messages.

While the tradition of assigning symbolism to flora dates back to Ancient Greece, where plants were seen to possess powers of sympathetic magic, and was later popular at the Ottoman and Elizabethan courts, it was in Victorian Britain that floriography became most highly systematized and widely popular. Victorian society, particularly those classes bound by formal codes of conduct, found an elegant outlet for creative expression in the language of flowers. This period saw the publication of many dictionaries and guidebooks devoted to the subject.

Each flower carried a specific meaning. For instance, roses were particularly nuanced in their symbolism. A red rose signified passionate love, while a white rose signified purity and innocence. Yellow roses could signify jealousy or infidelity, pink roses admiration and gratitude. Lilies signified purity and refined beauty. White lilies were a symbol of chastity and virtue. Daisies signified innocence and loyal love, violets modesty and faithfulness. Tulips varied in meaning based on their color: red tulips declared love, while yellow tulips suggested cheerful thoughts.

The nuances of floriography allowed for elaborate messages to be exchanged. A bouquet containing an assortment of flowers could communicate a detailed sentiment, with each flower adding another layer of meaning. Even the way flowers were placed held significance. An upright position generally indicated a positive sentiment, while a reversed flower suggested the opposite. A flower given with the right hand was viewed favorably, whereas the left hand might convey an unspoken warning or negative feeling.

Bouquets were carefully crafted to deliver specific messages. For example, a bouquet with forget-me-nots, ivy, and red roses might contain a plea for remembrance, eternal fidelity, and deep love, respectively.

The language of flowers extended beyond personal interactions to influence the arts, literature, and fashion of the nineteenth century. This built upon, but did not displace, a more expansive literary symbolism of flowers. In Emily Brontë's 1847 novel, *Wuthering Heights*, themes of untamed passion versus social propriety are contrasted in the wild, natural landscape of the moors and the cultivated flowers at Thrushcross Grange. In George Eliot's 1871 novel, *Middlemarch*, the flowers that surround Dorothea Brooke reflect her purity and idealism, while the flowers in Rosamond Vincy's environment reflect her superficial beauty and manipulative nature.[12]

Likewise, floral motifs in the visual arts were laden with significance. As an extension of their commitment to truth in nature, and their continued use of rich botanical ornamentation, derived from the gothic revival, the Pre-Raphaelite artists employed floral symbolism to a high degree.

A fine example of floriography can be found in Dante Gabriel Rossetti's painting, *Beata Beatrix*, completed in 1870. As mentioned in the previous chapter, this was a poignant homage to Rossetti's wife, Elizabeth Siddal, who died very young. The painting depicts her as Beatrice, from *La Vita Nuova* by Dante Alighieri.

What are the elements of the composition? A poppy flower, symbolizing sleep and death, is gently placed in Beatrice's hand by a red dove—the messenger of love—suggesting her transition from life to death. The use of the poppy, whose seed pod is the source of opium, the cause of Lizzie's death, connects the real to the idealized, mourning to memory, love to loss.

Rossetti's 1874 painting, *Proserpine*, portrays the Ancient Greek goddess Persephone, queen of the underworld, but also goddess of spring. She was the daughter of Demeter, the goddess of agriculture and fertility. Persephone was abducted by Hades, the god of the underworld. In her grief over the loss of her daughter, Demeter ignored the earth, causing crops to wither and the fields to become barren. Zeus, the king of the gods, alarmed by the suffering of mortals, intervened and brokered a deal: Persephone would spend part of the year with Hades in the underworld and the rest with her mother on earth. This compromise led to the creation of the seasons. When Persephone was in the underworld, Demeter mourned, and winter blanketed the earth. When Persephone returned, Demeter rejoiced, and spring brought renewal and growth. Thus, the myth of Persephone exemplifies the dying and reawakening of nature, in the cyclical pattern of the seasons. Rossetti's depiction includes a pomegranate, red like the lips of his model, Jane Morris, a fruit of fertility, abundance, but also, paradoxically, death. Surrounding Persephone, or Prosperine, as she was known to the Romans, are ivy leaves, like all evergreens a symbol of resurrection and eternal life.

As in *Beata Beatrix*, Rossetti seems to have used floriography in his 1880 painting, *The Day Dream*, to express matters close to his own heart. Here, Rossetti depicted Jane Morris, his muse of later years, holding in one hand a branch of sycamore, and in the other a sprig of honeysuckle. The sycamore symbolizes fidelity, an ironic choice given their complicated relationship, as Jane was married to William Morris, Rossetti's friend. The honeysuckle might also symbolize fidelity, or else sweetness and the bonds of love. The viewer may perceive in this selection of plants a tension between loyalty and desire in the triangle involving Rossetti and the Morrises.

There is, of course, a limit to the interpretive value of this system. It is only one lens through which floral symbolism in Victorian art can be viewed. Plants that blossom in certain seasons or conditions might be chosen to correspond with certain seasons or conditions of life. In some cases both meanings are layered. Consider John William Waterhouse's 1909 painting, *Gather Ye Rosebuds While Ye May*. It is an illustration of the seventeenth century poem, "To the Virgins, to Make Much of Time," by Robert Herrick. Both poem and painting admonish young ladies to take advantage of the springtime of life before the bloom of youth fades. But the rosebud specifically communicates love as the bounty to be harvested. Herrick wrote, "Then be not coy, but use your time, / And while ye may, go marry; / For having lost but once your prime, / You may forever tarry."[13] It is sufficient to acknowledge that the Pre-Raphaelite artists were aware of the language of flowers to apply this in greater or lesser extent as an interpretive tool.

William Holman Hunt combined floriography with biblical references to create potent botanical symbols of his own. These have been loaded into the background of his 1853 painting, *The Awakening Conscience*. Here, he captures a moment of sudden moral clarity experienced by a young woman, who is the kept mistress of a man that will not, or cannot, marry her. She is portrayed rising from the lap of her lover, who is in turn seated at a piano, her reflective gaze indicating the epiphany of her peril. The man's lustful, jocular expression reveals his own obliviousness to her enlightenment.

At first the eye is drawn to these central figures. But as the viewer investigates the surrounding scene, clues that have, perhaps, informed the woman's own self consciousness, can be found. The setting is a richly decorated room, filled with ornate furnishings: in this context a gilded cage of material comfort and spiritual emptiness. A mirror behind the woman reflects her view of a sunny garden outside, offering the path of repentance to a better, more virtuous life.

Frederic George Stephens, in his 1860 memoir of Hunt, observed that, "The very decorations on the wall are significant, and might have suggested repentance before." The pattern of the wallpaper depicts "a vineyard, in which corn is mingled with the vine; birds destroy the grapes of the latter, while at the foot sleeps a boy-guardian, whose horn, fallen from his hand, indicates neglected duty."[14] All throughout Holy Scripture, corn and new wine are given as typical of God's blessing. Isaac says to Jacob in Genesis 27:28, "Therefore God give thee of the dew of heaven, and the fatness of the earth, and plenty of corn and wine," a sentiment reiterated by Moses in Deuteronomy 33:28, when he gives his final prophesy that, "the fountain of Jacob shall be upon a land of corn and wine; also his heavens shall drop down dew." In Hunt's analogy, God's blessing has been squandered—even allowed to be poached—through ignorance of virtue.

Stephens was the only non-artist member of the Pre-Raphaelite Brotherhood, besides William Michael Rossetti. Later an art critic, Stephens was the close friend and champion of Hunt for many years. His proximity to the artist suggests familiarity with Hunt's authorial intent. So it is noteworthy that Stephens made direct reference to the lexicon of floriography in his description. He wrote that, "Upon the frame," constructed to display *Awakening Conscience*, "are ringing bells, and marigolds, the emblems of warning and sorrow."[15] Hunt included marigolds in the foreground of his 1851 painting, *The Hireling Shepherd*, an earlier study of the abandonment of duty, where they serve a similar purpose.

John Everett Millais's *Ophelia* is arguably the most accomplished floral painting in the Pre-Raphaelite corpus. His poignant depiction of Shakespeare's tragic character from *Hamlet* is an exercise in fidelity to the forms of nature. Millais's attention to detail and his adherence to the text make the painting a rich subject for both art and literary analysis.

In *Hamlet*, Act 4, Scene 5, Ophelia's descent into madness is communicated through floriography. Shakespeare gave no stage directions for the scene, but it is always played with Ophelia handing out flowers to the other characters as she speaks:

OPHELIA: There's rosemary, that's for remembrance. Pray you, love, remember. And there is pansies, that's for thoughts.

LAERTES: A document in madness: thoughts and remembrance fitted.

OPHELIA: There's fennel for you, and columbines. There's rue for you, and here's some for me; we may call it herb of grace o' Sundays. You must wear your rue with a difference. There's a daisy. I would give you some violets, but they withered all when my father died. They say he made a good end.[16]

Shakespeare selected these plants to illustrate themes of betrayal, vengeance, and sorrow that permeate the play. Each flower carries a weight of symbolic meaning. To her brother Laertes, she gives the rosemary and pansies, for remembrance and thoughts, respectively. The audience understands that he is bidden to remember their father, Polonius, who was killed by Hamlet while hiding behind a curtain, to eavesdrop. Laertes's remembrance of this act culminates in the duel that kills both Hamlet and himself. The fennel and columbines are given to King Claudius, who murdered Hamlet's father, and married his mother. Stephanie Chatfield interprets these elements of the bouquet in her essay, "Ophelia's Flowers," writing, "Fennel for flattery. Columbine may mean ingratitude. Fennel was also believed to cast away evil spirits. Perhaps Ophelia was suggesting that Claudius was evil." The rue is given to Queen Gertrude. Chatfield suggests, "Rue for repentance. Is the queen to wear hers with a difference because she shows no repentance for her previous husband's death?"[17] The dramaturg Lydia Grabau writes that, traditionally, "Ophelia picks up and sets down the daisy without giving it to anyone. This is interesting because the daisy is the symbol of innocence and gentleness. Evidently Ophelia thought there was no place for innocence" at the doomed court.[18] Finally, the association of violets with faithfulness can be seen to carry the reverse connotation, as they have withered. The element is therefore missing in the relationships between the characters in the play.

Millais included all of these flowers in his painting, as well as others named in Act 4, Scene 7. Relating news of Ophelia's death, Queen Gertrude describes the former as having woven "fantastic garlands" out of "crow-flowers, nettles, daisies, and long purples that liberal shepherds give a grosser name, but our cold maids do dead men's fingers call them."[19] Millais depicted most of the flowers strewn about Ophelia's body, or in the water, floating away. Some he painted growing along the banks, including the long purples. These Millais interpreted as purple loosestrife, though they are elsewhere cited as orchids.

Millais did not restrict himself entirely to the flowers mentioned in *Hamlet*. He also painted the flora growing naturally in the landscape of the Hogsmill River where he laid out the background. These extra-textual additions have their own significance: the poppy for sleep and death, forget-me-nots for remembrance, roses for love and beauty.

Because Millais painted the same landscape over a period of five months, he captured flowers that blossomed at intervals throughout the year, next to one another in full bloom simultaneously. For example purple loosestrife blossoms in late summer or fall, forget-me-nots in spring. The presence of these flowers, out of season, creates a timeless and dreamlike quality, underscoring the otherworldly tragedy of Ophelia's demise.

The result of Millais's painstaking process was a lush botanical scene rendered with scientific precision. A reviewer for the *Athenaeum* likened it to a "study of Linnaeus' saturated with a Protestant work ethic." John Guille Millais related perhaps "the greatest compliment ever paid" to his father's painting, "as regards its truthfulness to Nature," when "a certain Professor of Botany, being unable to take his class into the country" for fieldwork, "took them" instead "to the Guildhall," where *Ophelia* "was being exhibited, and discoursed to them upon the flowers and plants before them, which were, he said, as instructive as Nature herself."[20] In his 1911 biography of Millais, John Ernest Phythian concluded that, "The story is more than credible. The picture compels us to believe it."[21] Indeed.

Even the painting's detractors were struck by its composition. A reviewer for *The Times* at *Ophelia*'s debut in 1852, wrote of the artist, "there must be something strangely perverse in an imagination which souses Ophelia in a weedy ditch," stripping "all pathos and beauty" from "the drowning struggle of that lovelorn maiden" while at the same time, "it studies every petal of the darnel and anemone floating on the eddy and pricks out a robin on the pollard from which Ophelia fell."[22]

The juxtaposition of life and death—death in life? life surrounding death?—has a startling quality. Writing in the journal, *Romantik*, Peter Brix Søndergaard refers to the "Shakespearian erotic death or 'love death'" depicted in the painting. He observes that to the left of the forget-me-nots in the background, "we see a configuration of light and shadow vaguely resembling a skull." He suggests that this "common *memento mori* may refer to both Ophelia's death and the famous graveyard scene that follows" in the next act of the play.[23]

The stark contrast between subject and setting can be viewed in several different ways. Of course, Ophelia, with her pale, inert form floating amidst abundant flora, embodies the tragedy of untimely death—she has been cut down in the bloom of life. The flora in its riotous growth displays nature's indifferent beauty. Millais suggests that the transience of human existence takes place within the context of nature's perpetual renewal. However obliquely, the giving way of death to life in nature must also stand as a symbol of Christian resurrection.

III. 'MIGHT I HAVE A BIT OF EARTH':

An allegorical interpretation of Victorian horticulture can be found in Frances Hodgson Burnett's novel *The Secret Garden*. Written at the end of the Edwardian era, it tells the story of a young English girl, Mary, who is sent to live with her uncle at his estate, Misselthwaite Manor, in Yorkshire, after her parents die in India. Her uncle, Mr Craven, is frequently absent and Mary is left to her own devises. Exploring the grounds of the house she discovers a walled garden that has been locked. She learns that her aunt died in an accident in the garden years before and her uncle had it closed off in his grief. With the help of a local boy named Dickon, she opens the garden and begins to tend it. Meanwhile at night Mary hears mysterious cries coming from somewhere in the manor. She searches the halls by candlelight and discovers her cousin Colin, a sickly boy confined to his bed, and treated as a hopeless invalid by the servants.[24]

What thus begins as a gothic novel with all the classic elements of the genre soon blossoms into something entirely different. In her essay, "Re-Reading *The Secret Garden*," Madelon Gohlke writes, "The conversations between Mary and the uncanny Colin in which she systematically opposes his conviction that he is going to die parallel the coming of spring and the awakening of life in the garden." Mary and Dickon draw Colin out of his sick bed and into the garden where the three children spend an idyllic season and nature works to restore them body and soul together with the vegetation. Mr Craven returns to find his son healthy and the garden in bloom. Gohlke write, "At the center of this image, of course, is the garden, the place where the secrets of life, growth, and all the richness of feeling are located and then revealed." The garden "is both the scene of a tragedy, resulting in the near destruction of a family, and the place of regeneration and restoration of a family."[25]

These were the ideas associated with gardening, then as now: the symbiotic relationship between man and nature, its cycles, and its latent spirituality.

CHAPTER FOUR

DEATH AND RESURRECTION

At an early meeting of the Pre-Raphaelite Brotherhood, in 1848, the young artists made a record of the historical figures who had influenced the movement. "We, the undersigned, declare that the following list of Immortals constitutes the whole of our Creed," wrote Dante Gabriel Rossetti, as scribe, "and that there exists no other Immortality than what is centred in their names and in the names of their contemporaries, in whom this list is reflected."[1] They went on to name various important personages, drawn mostly from art, literature, and statecraft.

Jesus Christ was given first place on the list, followed by the author of the Book of Job, and the prophet Isaiah. From all of classical antiquity two names were selected: the poet Homer and the sculptor Pheidias, whose decorative stonework, from the frieze on the Parthenon in Athens, had come to the British Museum earlier in the nineteenth century, as the centerpiece of the Elgin Marbles. The Middle Ages were represented broadly, by the "Early Gothic Architects" and the "Early English Balladists." Dante Alighieri and Geoffrey Chaucer were mentioned by name. At the Renaissance, the list became more detailed, including most of the principle Italian painters up to —and indeed, beyond—Raphael. Of the Baroque masters, whose influence over contemporary art the Pre-Raphaelites opposed, only Nicolas Poussin was deemed worthy. The virtues of the English political order, with its Gothic Constitution, were summarized by King Alfred the Great and Oliver Cromwell. From the seventeenth century onward, almost all of the "Immortals" were British, with the exception of Johann Wolfgang von Goethe and a number of American poets. The English Renaissance contributed Sir Francis Bacon, William Shakespeare, Edmund Spenser, and John Milton. The neoclassical period contributed Sir Isaac Newton, William Hogarth, John Flaxman, and Sir David Wilkie. The Romantic movement contributed William Wordsworth, Samuel Taylor Coleridge, William Savage Landor, Leigh Hunt, Benjamin Haydon, William Hilton, Lord Byron, Percy Bysshe Shelley, John Keats, Ralph Waldo Emerson, Henry Wadsworth Longfellow, and Edgar Allan Poe. The list was brought up to date with an earlier generation of Victorians, including, Charles Jeremiah Wells, credited as the author of *Stories After Nature*, Lord Tennyson, the Brownings, and Coventry Patmore.[2]

The names do not appear to be arranged in any particular order. It is easy to imagine Rossetti writing them down as they were proposed and approved by the group in one spontaneous exercise. There is a somewhat arbitrary quality to the list that would support that image. People who obviously influenced the group are conspicuously absent, while others, with no discernible connection, are included. But overall the list provides a useful foundation for the Pre-Raphaelite movement. According to William Holman Hunt, an earlier draft "included further names than those in the present copy, amongst them many contemporaries now utterly forgotten."[3]

In his memoir, *Pre-Raphaelitism and the Pre-Raphaelite Brotherhood*, Hunt took pains to correct any misconception, gleaned from the document, that the artists were irreligious. He communicated Rossetti's expressions of "astonishment made in his last years that men should assume that he denied an after life," whereas everything Rossetti "had painted and written ought to convince them of his belief in immortality." For his own part, "not many weeks after signing this document," Hunt began work on the painting, *A Converted British Family Sheltering a Christian Missionary from the Persecution of the Druids*, which he undertook in honor of the "obedience to Christ's command that His doctrine should be preached to all the world at the expense of life itself."[4]

It is not immediately apparent why the association of immortality with Jesus Christ and the great men of European arts and letters would be confused for a statement of nihilism. Perhaps the implication was that fame itself is the only lasting monument. Hunt's confession of faith speaks for itself. In fact, the Pre-Raphaelites possessed an impressive understanding of Christian eschatology as regards the hope of the world to come.

The artists and poets associated with the group were by no means uniform in their religious outlook, but they shared a seriousness of purpose that often led them to engage—directly or obliquely—with Christian themes. Even where doctrinal belief was uncertain or idiosyncratic, the imaginative structure of Christian theology continued to shape their symbolic language. This is especially true of works that confront death, judgment, and the promise of eternal life—themes that appear with notable frequency across both canvas and page. Of all those linked to the movement, it was Christina Rossetti who engaged most profoundly with these questions, doing so with a theological orthodoxy often absent from her brother Dante's treatments of the theme. An appreciation of several important works of Pre-Raphaelite poetry depends upon an understanding of certain fundamental points of Christian belief. For this reason, a concise summary will be helpful.

I. THE RESURRECTION OF THE BODY:

During the Babylonian captivity, when the Kingdom of Judah was destroyed, and its nobility sent into exile throughout the empire, God vouchsafed to the prophet Ezekiel certain visions of Israel restored. Judah was the last of the old Kingdom of Israel. The northern tribes had rebelled against the royal line of King David and raised their own kings. These tribes had fallen to Assyria more than a century earlier and had been driven from the Holy Land. Now the Kingdom of Judah was lost as well. In this time of grief, God made a promise to Ezekiel. It was a promise to restore Israel, but it contained another, greater promise, that would be fulfilled through Jesus Christ: a promise to bring the dead back to life.

Ezekiel said, "The hand of the Lord came upon me and brought me out in the Spirit of the Lord, and set me down in the midst of the valley; and it was full of bones. Then He caused me to pass by them all around, and behold, there were very many in the open valley; and indeed they were very dry."

God asked, "Son of man, can these bones live?"

Ezekiel answered, "O Lord God, You know."

God then commanded, "Prophesy to these bones, and say to them, 'O dry bones, hear the word of the Lord! Thus says the Lord God to these bones: Surely I will cause breath to enter into you, and you shall live. I will put sinews on you and bring flesh upon you, cover you with skin and put breath in you; and you shall live. Then you shall know that I am the Lord.'"[5]

As He did for those bones, God would do for the Kingdom

of Judah, and as He did for those bones, God will do for each and every individual man and woman who has ever lived. One of the essential doctrines of Christian faith is the general Resurrection of the Dead. The Christian hope is not for a disembodied "afterlife" but for life restored. The Christian does not believe, with the Ancient Greeks, that the soul lives on only as a shade in the Underworld. Christians do not believe, with the Eastern religions, that the soul reincarnates in a succession of different bodies over time. Christians believe that a day will come when the earth is made new again, and the tombs are broken open, and the dead are raised up in their original bodies to real, physical life by God. This belief is predicated upon the incarnation, death, and resurrection of Jesus Christ. In Christ, God was born a man, died nailed to the cross as a man, and was raised again to eternal life in the flesh as a man. By his conquest of death Christ made it possible that mortal men and women will return from their own deaths to life.

The doctrine of the Resurrection of the Dead has been affirmed by Christians, in all denominations, from apostolic times to the present. In the Gospel of Matthew, Christ uses the phrase, ἀναστάσεως τῶν νεκρῶν to describe the phenomenon: the "raising up"—literally the "standing up again"—of the dead. The general resurrection is among the wonders, terrors, and glories of the end times, foretold by John in the Book of Revelation. "For the trumpet will sound," the Apostle Paul wrote in his first letter to the Corinthians, "and the dead will be raised incorruptible, and we shall be changed."[6] Paul emphasized the indispensability of this doctrine, writing to the Corinthians, "if the dead are not raised, then Christ has not been raised. If Christ has not been raised, your faith is futile and you are still in your sins."[7]

The Church Fathers were adamant on the subject. Justin

Martyr wrote, "Indeed, God calls even the body to resurrection and promises it everlasting life. When he promises to save the man, he thereby makes his promise to the flesh."[8] Theophilus of Antioch taught that, "God will raise up your flesh immortal with your soul."[9] Irenaeus proclaimed, "the raising up again of all flesh of all humanity."[10]

Tertullian and Augustine elaborated on what resurrection would entail. Tertullian wrote, "Therefore, the flesh shall rise again: certainly of every man, certainly the same flesh, and certainly in its entirety. Wherever it is, it is in safekeeping with God through that most faithful agent between God and man, Jesus Christ, who shall reconcile both God to man and man to God, the spirit to the flesh and the flesh to the spirit."[11] No matter how long the body has laid in the ground, or what is left of it, Augustine affirmed that "the omnipotence of the Creator" is able, "for the raising of our bodies and for the restoring of them to life, to recall all parts, which were consumed by beasts or by fire, or which disintegrated into dust or ashes, or were melted away into a fluid, or were evaporated away in vapors."[12]

The Church Fathers spoke with absolute clarity and literalness on this doctrine because it was a point of distinction from other religions in Late Antiquity. The Ancient Greeks had a traditional belief in bodily resurrection, attributing physical immortality to their great heroes, as attested by Homer and Hesiod. By the classical period, however, this belief had been undermined. Under the influence of the Pharisees, the Jews also had become ambivalent about the doctrine of resurrection by the time of the coming of Christ.

For this reason the Church Fathers reiterated, again and again, in the creeds and in their personal writings, the doctrine of resurrection. They emphasized that resurrection was a literal physical process; it was not a metaphor or a mystery. As the Anglican theologian N.T. Wright explains in his commentary, *Revelation for Everyone*: "Resurrection, in the first-century world, emphatically meant the undoing of death, not its reinterpretation. It meant that the processes of bodily corruption and decay were reversed, producing a new 'physical' body with 'immortal' properties."[13] In other words, the resurrected person would be the same person who died, made of the same genetic material, transformed, perfected, but not less or other than he or she was.

The Protestant Reformers of the sixteenth century likewise advanced the same doctrine. Martin Luther described the physicality of resurrection, writing, "For thus it has pleased God to raise up from worms, from corruption, from the earth, which is totally putrid and full of stench, a body more beautiful than any flower, than balsam, than the sun itself and the stars."[14] In the English Church, Thomas Cranmer, the first Protestant Archbishop of Canterbury, and the principal author of *The Book of Common Prayer*, elaborated at length on the subject of bodily resurrection. Cranmer reconciled the Apostle Paul's distinction between spirit and flesh, writing:

I know that St Paul saith that in the resurrection our bodies shall be spiritual, meaning in the respect of such vileness, filthiness, sin, and corruption, as we be subject unto in this miserable world: yet he saith not that our bodies shall be all spiritual. For notwithstanding such spiritualness as St Paul speaketh of, we shall have all such substantial parts and members as pertain to a very natural man's body. So that in this part our bodies shall be carnal, corporal, real, and natural bodies, lacking nothing that belongeth to perfect men's bodies. And in that respect is the body of Christ also carnal, and not spiritual.[15]

Cranmer defines this carnality in detail. He explains that Christ's risen body "hath the same flesh and natural substance which was born of the virgin Mary" and that "his natural body now glorified hath all the natural parts of a man's body in order, proportion, and place distinct, as our bodies shall be in these respects carnal after our resurrection."[16]

Today there is widespread ignorance about the doctrine of resurrection. In 2006 the Scripps Survey Research Center at Ohio University asked 1,007 American adults the following question: "Do you believe that, after you die, your physical body will be resurrected someday?" In a country that over-whelmingly professes the Christian faith, 54 percent answered "no." Only 44 percent of Protestants and 38 percent of Roman Catholics answered "yes."[17]

Opinion surveys should be read with skepticism. One thousand random people cannot speak for hundreds of millions. On the other hand these findings are entirely plausi-ble. If one knew nothing about Christian eschatology, what would one learn about it from casual contact with twenty-first century religion? One might come away with a general impres-sion of the afterlife involving the survival of the soul in a disembodied state forever: "in heaven," perhaps, with harps, clouds, and angel wings. Many well-meaning people seem to believe this. But it is not a Christian belief.

The general confusion about the nature of the life to come reflects a corresponding confusion about the nature of the human person. According to Christianity neither the soul nor the body alone is the person, only together. On this point, Christians have always agreed with Aristotle. Anthony Kenny paraphrases the Aristotelian view in his *New History of Western Philosophy*, writing, "If one regards a living substance as a composite of matter and form, then the soul is the form of a natural organic body."[18] The purpose and destiny of the soul is to impose upon matter the specific form of the individual human person.

When we speak of the survival of the soul we are speaking of the preservation of the soul from death. The soul is preserved by God not as an end unto itself. The unique "form" of a man is preserved so that it can reconstitute the whole: the living, physical, man—body, mind, and soul. Incidentally, this is why Eastern doctrines of reincarnation, also called metempsychosis, are impossible: the soul can regenerate the same form but it cannot generate different forms or different persons.

Christianity does, of course, teach the survival of the soul. In the intermediary space between death and resurrection are all the mysteries of the human *psyche* and its place in the spiritual architecture of Creation. But that is secondary. Scripture offers very little detail. In an interview with *Time* magazine, Wright explained, "We know that we will be with God and with Christ, resting and being refreshed. Paul writes that it will be conscious, but compared with being bodily alive, it will be like being asleep." Scripture is far more concerned with what Wright calls, "life *after* life after death."[19]

The materiality of the world to come, described in the Book of Revelation, provides a stark contrast to the unbiblical notion that the righteous dead "go to heaven" when they die. As J. Richard Middleton writes, "There is not one single reference in the entire biblical canon...to heaven as the eternal destiny of the believer."[20] According to Scripture, mankind does not *go to heaven*, but rather, *heaven comes to mankind*. Revelation depicts the renewal of earth to the condition of Eden and the return of Christ to reign as its high king. A New Jerusalem is depicted as descending upon our sphere of Creation to be the metropole of a New Earth. Based on the vast dimensions of the city, this New Earth is exponentially larger than the fallen earth. It contains nations with kings and lands. Revelation describes "a pure river" of "the water of life, clear as crystal" flowing out of the New Jerusalem. "In the midst of the street of it, and on either side of the river" the Tree of Life grows, "which bare twelve manner of fruits," yielding "her fruit every month: and the leaves of the tree were for the healing of the nations."[21] The gates of the city are never closed and "the kings of the earth do bring their glory and honour into it."[22] With these verses, Revelation offers a peripheral glimpse of the nations of the resurrected, living in lands that are cognate to their historic realms, carrying on the project of redeemed humanity forever.

II. 'WHEN DUST REANIMATE BEGINS TO STIR':

Victorian religion was not immune from the issues found by the Scripps survey among present-day Christians. In his book, *Breathers of an Ampler Day: Victorian Views of Heaven*, Ian Bradley identifies a "tendency towards universalism, emphasis on immortality rather than resurrection," and "lack of focus on judgment," which, though not necessarily dominant, certainly affected popular faith across denominations in the nineteenth century.[23] Brian Castle writes, in his book, *Sing a New Song to the Lord*, that, "There was a preference for the immortality of the soul rather than the resurrection of the body in the Victorian understanding of the afterlife."[24] Castle based his analysis on a study of Victorian hymns. But in the popular songs and sermons of the nineteenth century there were also clear expressions of doctrinal orthodoxy on the subject of the general resurrection. Victorians were certainly as well—if not better—catechized on the subject as their twenty-first century counterparts.

Consider two famous Anglican hymns of the period: "Resurrection Morn," written in 1866 by Sabine Baring-Gould, the prolific folklorist and clergyman, or "Alleluia! Alleluia!," written in 1872 by Christopher Wordsworth, younger brother to the poet laureate, who was Bishop of Lincoln. Baring-Gould's funerary hymn describes the transition of the afterlife from death to resurrection. The opening stanzas read:

> On the resurrection morning
>> Soul and body meet again;
>> No more sorrow, no more weeping,
>> No more pain.
>
> Here awhile they must be parted,
>> And the flesh its sabbath keep,
>> Waiting in a holy stillness,
>> Wrapt in sleep.
>
> For a space that tired body
>> Lies with feet toward the dawn;
>> Till there breaks the last and brightest
>> Easter morn.
>
> But the soul in contemplation
>> Utters earnest prayers and strong;
>> Breaking at the resurrection
>> Into song.
>
> Soul and body reunited,
>> Thenceforth nothing will divide,
>> Waking up in Christ's own likeness,
>> Satisfied.[25]

The presentation of the subject matter, with its emphasis on patient waiting, is reminiscent of the treatment of death in the poems of Christina Rossetti. Like any good funerary hymn, it doubles as an Easter song. Wordsworth's hymn was written specifically for Easter day. Its subject is the Savior's triumph over death, through which, "we with Him to life eternal by His resurrection rise." The third stanza proclaims:

> Christ is risen, Christ, the first-fruits
> of the holy harvest field,
> which will all its full abundance
> at His second coming yield.
> Then the golden ears of harvest
> will their heads before Him wave,
> ripened by His glorious sunshine
> from the furrows of the grave.[26]

To the credit of the Victorians, not only did they produce hymns such as these, that reinforced correct doctrine, they attempted some degree of institutional pushback against the type that did not. The publishers of *Hymns Ancient and Modern*, the most widely used hymnal in the Church of England, during the late nineteenth century, were evidently aware of the trend later noticed by Castle. When a revised edition was planned in the 1890s, a sub-committee for "Hymns on Heaven and Kindred Subjects" was convened to advise the editors. The group issued the following statement:

> there is no scriptural warrant for assuming that any of the departed Saints are risen or will rise from the dead before the General Resurrection on the Last Day; or that it is possible for human beings to enter into a full fruition of heavenly blessedness without the Resurrection of the Body. We should not wish, therefore, to see the book include any hymns which appear distinctly to teach the contrary.[27]

Because hymns serve an instructional, as well as devotional, purpose, their content can offer insight into popular theology. What can we learn about the Pre-Raphaelites from the way they worshipped? In the case of Christina Rossetti, much insight can be gleaned.

The Rossetti family attended Christ Church, St Pancras in Albany Street beginning around 1843. They had previously attended Holy Trinity, Marylebone and St Katherine's Chapel, Regent's Park. Christ Church was a new parish, founded six years earlier, in part with funds from Edward Pusey, the leading figure in the Oxford Movement of the Church of England. The Oxford Movement was a faction within the Protestant national church that emphasized the medieval inheritance of the Anglican tradition. At its best the movement inspired ministries to the poor and encouraged the gothic revival through patronage. Its apologists demonstrated that Anglicanism had a claim to unbroken continuity with the ancient universal church, equal to the claims of Roman Catholicism and Eastern Orthodoxy. At its worst the movement sought to displace authentic Anglican forms, based on organic tradition and Reformation theology, with the liturgical trappings of nineteenth-century Roman Catholicism; in this it certainly did more harm than good. Christ Church was intended to be a showcase for the Oxford Movement. It was the first such parish outside of Oxford itself. But the project began disastrously. The initial incumbent, William Dodsworth, converted to Roman Catholicism in 1851, abandoning the parish. After the scandal of Dodsworth's apostasy, Henry William Burroughs was appointed perpetual curate. Under Burroughs the parish achieved stability, though it never became the model church that Pusey had hoped.

The Oxford Movement must have appealed to the unique circumstances of the Rossetti siblings. Their mother Frances

Polidori was Protestant. Their father Gabriele Rossetti had arrived in England from Italy as a political exile. He was a major figure in the movement which sought to unite the divided states of the Italian peninsula into one nation, an objective ultimately accomplished by the Risorgimento of 1861. William Michael Rossetti described his father as being "a nominal Roman Catholic" who was "vehemently opposed to all papal and sacerdotal pretensions" and "dissented altogether" from the "ecclesiastical dogmas" of the Roman Church.[28] The anti-papal character of the Italian national heroes is well known. General Garibaldi was attended by a Protestant chaplain. Many of the leaders of the Risorgimento were Freemasons, an organization proscribed by the Church of Rome.

The Rossetti siblings had been raised Protestant in an Italian cultural environment. William Michael Rossetti wrote that it was "hardly an exaggeration to say that every Italian staying in or passing through London, of a Liberal mode of political opinion, sought out" his father, "to make or renew acquaintance with him."[29] This included figures ranging from Giuseppe Mazzini to the violinist Niccolò Paganini. In addition to dignitaries, biographer A.C. Benson described, "a perpetual flow of foreigners requiring assistance, and if a Masonic signal was given, Gabriele Rossetti being a Freemason, they were immediately relieved."[30] In this context, the Oxford Movement provided a religious arrangement seemingly designed for the Rossetti family: Italianate ritual in a Protestant church.

Despite the eclectic influences of both the Oxford Movement and the Pre-Raphaelite aesthetic, it should be understood that the religion of the Rossetti household was staunchly Anglican. The Roman Catholic artist James Collinson was obliged to convert to the Church of England in order to pursue his ultimately unsuccessful courtship of Christina Rossetti.

Lorraine Janzen Kooistra writes that Christina was comforted that her father's later writings "gave evidence" of his "turning to the Protestant faith in his last years."[31] Selections from Professor Rossetti's final posthumous volume of verse, *L'Arpa Evangelica*, or, *The Evangelical Harp*, became part of the "hymnology of Italian Evangelical churches," according to Rodolphe Louis Mégroz.[32]

Christina Rossetti, her mother Frances, her sister Maria, and her aunt, Eliza Polidori, were all members of the congregation at Christ Church, St Pancras. Dante Gabriel Rossetti designed a sequence of three stained glass windows depicting *The Sermon on the Mount* for the church. The windows, which were fabricated by Morris & Co., were installed in the 1860s when Christ Church was renovated by the gothic revival architect William Butterfield. "Within this environment," writes Emma Mason, in her spiritual biography of Christina Rossetti, the poet "attended Morning Prayer and Evening Prayer or Holy Communion, both of which were structured by sung psalms, a reading of the Ten Commandments...a prayer or collect, hymns, a sung Nicene Creed, and a sermon."[33] In 1855, shortly after he took up residence as curate, Reverend Burroughs published a collection of the hymns sung regularly at these services, entitled, *Hymns for Use in Church*.

Like the editors of *Hymns Ancient and Modern*, Reverend Burroughs drew significantly from the *Lyra Germanica*. This German hymnal, compiled for the Protestant churches of Prussia, by the diplomat and scholar Christian Charles Josias von Bunsen, had been translated into English by Catherine Winkworth in 1854. Two hymns in particular, taken from this volume, that were sung at Albany Street, deal with the general resurrection in bold physical terms.

The hymn numbered 117 in Reverend Burroughs's collection contains the prayer, "And let the earth my body keep, / Till the Last Day shall break its sleep." The hymn numbered 118, to be sung at a funeral, proclaims of the deceased, "His body reverently we bear, / It is not dead, but rests in God, / And softly sleeps beneath the sod." A recognition of the full physical reality of death gives way to the physicality of new life: "It seems as all were over now— / The heavy limbs, the soulless brow— / Yet through these rigid limbs once more / A nobler life ere long, shall pour." The hymn references the same passage from Ezekiel quoted above, continuing: "These dead, dry bones again shall feel / New warmth and vigour through them steal; / Reknit and living they shall soar / On high where Christ lives evermore."[34] That prophesy from Ezekiel seems to have occupied a significant place in Christina Rossetti's own religious imagination.

In her book, *The Face of the Deep: A Devotional Commentary on the Apocalypse*, Miss Rossetti wrote: "Ezekiel in three successive chapters...sets before us in vision or in prophesy a resurrection to life of perished Israel, and an upsurging and destruction of Gog with the hosts of Magog." Here again is the same passage quoted above. She interprets the prophesy with the same hermeneutics as the writer of Hymn 118, explaining, "However these three chapters may admit of previous temporal interpretation, they exhibit no less a vivid symbol of events which will close time and open eternity."[35] To wit, the general resurrection.

The promise of a physical rising from the dead was a matter of practical faith in the Rossetti household, at least among its pious women. In her memoir *Time Flies*, Christina recounts how her sister Maria "shrank from entering the Mummy Room at the British Museum under a vivid realisation of how the general resurrection might occur even as one stood among those solemn corpses turned into a sight for sightseers."[36] The sisters were encouraged in this, as in all matters of faith, by their mother. In his biography of Christina, Mackenzie Bell quotes an 1883 letter in which Miss Rossetti writes that Gabriel, who had died the previous year, "was a beloved, loving, conspicuous son of a widow, who cherishes among her dearest hopes that of receiving him back at the general Resurrection by the overflowing mercy of God."[37] With this in mind, Christina proposed the "Raising of the Widow Nain's Son" for the subject of a memorial window at Birchington Church, where Dante was buried, although another design was chosen.

As the longest-lived of the Rossetti siblings William Michael served as the literary executor for both Gabriel and Christina. Although himself an agnostic, William took great care to accurately and precisely describe his sister's religious beliefs. In the introduction to a 1904 edition of her poems, he observed that her writings "contemplate (in accordance with a dominant form of Christian belief) an 'intermediate state' of perfect rest and inchoate beatific vision before the day of judgement and the resurrection of the body" to eternal life. He concluded that for Christina, as a poet, at least, "an aspiration for rest after the turmoil of this mundane life is more marked than the yearning for heavenly bliss."[38] Certainly this intermediary period was the subject of many of her poems, including the selections in the Pre-Raphaelite journal, *The Germ*.

Ian Bradley writes that Miss Rossetti emphasized the need for the dead "to wait for the second coming of Christ, the last judgement and the general resurrection at the end of time" which, he argues, she reconciled with "the idea of the 'soul sleep', a long period of suspended animation after death in which souls rest". He describes how she "captures its dream-like state where there is a suspension of feeling and a kind of ambivalence between remembering and forgetting, but no cause for sadness or mourning among those left behind."[39]

William Michael Rossetti clarified to Mackenzie Bell: "You see Christina does not say there will not be recognition after the Resurrection, for then she was quite certain there would be recognition. She only expresses uncertainty on the point during the intermediate state after death and before the resurrection."[40] The intermediary state of death serves as a calm pause before the crescendo of the resurrection with its coming-in-again of life and consciousness and memory.

Miss Rossetti's poetic treatment of the subject was influenced not only by hymnody, but also by the visual arts. She cited an illustration by William Blake as being particularly important. In her memoir, *Time Flies*, Miss Rossetti wrote, "There is a design by William Blake symbolic of the Resurrection. In it I behold the descending soul and the arising body rushing together in an indissoluble embrace: and this design, among all I recollect to have seen, stands alone in expressing the rapture of that reunion."[41] The illustration is titled, appropriately, *The Reunion of the Soul & the Body*. It was originally engraved in 1813 as one of a series to accompany Robert Blair's poem, "The Grave."

Blake's influence on Miss Rossetti is not unexpected, as he was the subject of scholarly interest by her brothers, who were largely responsible for how Blake was received by the Victorians, and thus for his enduring reputation. Dante Gabriel Rossetti had acquired Blake's notebook in 1847. The book had been left by Blake's widow to his student Samuel Palmer. Palmer's brother sold it to Rossetti for ten shillings. In 1850 Rossetti transcribed and edited the notebook, extracting forty-two poems and fragments. The notebook was rebound together with Rossetti's thirty-three page appendix, including the note, "All that is of any value in the foregoing pages has here been copied out. D.G. C. R."[42] The entire document is known to this day as *The Rossetti Manuscript*. Dante and

William Rossetti were both involved in the publication of Alexander Gilchrist's important biography, *Life of William Blake*. When Gilchrist died in 1861, the book was still unfinished. The Rossetti brothers assisted Gilchrist's widow in completing the work from the author's notes. When the *Life of William Blake* was published in 1863, it included a selection of poetry and prose edited by Dante, including twenty-nine previously unpublished poems taken from the notebook. William Michael Rossetti annotated the 1863 edition, as Martin Butlin observed, in an article for *Blake: An Illustrated Quarterly*, with "additional entries, corrections and dates, notes of condition and so on," that were included in the 1880 edition.[43] The publishers George Bell and Frederick Daldy subsequently invited William Rossetti to edit the 1874 Aldine edition of the *Poetical Works of William Blake*.

In the 1911 doctoral thesis, *William Blake in his Relation to Dante Gabriel Rossetti*, J.C.E. Bassalik-de Vries wrote that, "The influence which William Blake exercised on Dante Gabriel Rossetti was of a three-fold nature." First, "as a philosopher," second, "as a poet," and third, "as a painter."[44] The first two may equally apply to Christina.

The most comprehensive statement of Miss Rossetti's faith in the resurrection of the body appears in her posthumously published poem, "By Way of Remembrance," which appeared first in the preface to the 1904 edition of her *Poetical Works*. Christina wrote:

In Resurrection is it awfuller
    That rising of the All or of the Each—
    Of all kins, of all nations, of all speech,
   Or one by one of him and him and her?
   When dust reanimate begins to stir
    Here, there, beyond, beyond, reach beyond reach;

> While every wave disgorges on its beach,
> Alive or dead-in-life, some seafarer.
> In Resurrection, on the day of days,
> That day of mourning throughout all the earth,
> In Resurrection may we meet again:
> No more with stricken hearts to part in twain;
> As once in sorrow one, now one in mirth,
> One in our resurrection-songs of praise.[45]

Here we find the stark—even shocking—fleshliness of the resurrection articulated also in Ezekiel's prophesy of sinews re-knitting over bones. The image of waves disgorging the bodies of those lost at sea upon the beach at various stages of resurrection is taken from a prophesy of the final judgement in the book of Revelation: "And the sea gave up the dead which were in it; and death and hell delivered up the dead which were in them" to the judgement of God.[46] This same passage was the subject of a painting by Frederic, Lord Leighton, whose career was connected with—and adjacent to—that of the Pre-Raphaelite Brotherhood.

III. AND THE SEA GAVE UP THE DEAD:

Lord Leighton was a distinguished British painter and sculptor of the Victorian era, principally associated with the Aesthetic Movement and Academic art. Born in Scarborough, England, in 1830, he was of a generation with the Pre-Raphaelites, being a year and a half younger than Millais. He displayed an early talent for art, which was nurtured by his wealthy family. Leighton's father was a doctor and his grandfather had been the personal physician to the Tsars of Russia. Leighton traveled extensively across Europe in his youth. Having been educated at the Academy of Fine Arts in Florence, he moved to London in

1860, a full decade after the controversies surrounding the Royal Academy exhibition of 1850.

Lord Leighton had a noteworthy, if somewhat indirect relationship with the Pre-Raphaelite artists. He shared their interest in meticulous detail, vibrant color, and themes derived from literature and history. Leighton traveled in the same social circles as Millais and Hunt, and considered them friends, although their artistic philosophies diverged in certain key ways. Unlike the Pre-Raphaelites, who challenged academic norms with their early emphasis on realism and medievalism, Leighton worked firmly within the traditions of Academic art, emphasizing classical idealism and elegance. Nonetheless, elements of the Pre-Raphaelite style, particularly that bold use of color and attention to nature, can be seen in Leighton's work. Paintings such as *Flaming June* and *The Garden of the Hesperides*, suggest a synthesis between Academic classicism and the romanticism of the Pre-Raphaelites. In this way Leighton typified the nascent Aesthetic Movement which developed out of the convergence of those two artistic streams.

Like Waterhouse or Alma-Tadema, Leighton seemed at times to "converse" with the Pre-Raphaelites through the figurative and scenic arrangements in his work. His 1871 painting, *After Vespers*, could have been designed, though not painted, by Rossetti. The composition directly echoes the narrative female portraits that Rossetti was producing during the same period with Alexa Wilding and Jane Morris. Leighton's contribution to the 1866 Royal Academy show, *The Painter's Honeymoon*, is likewise harmonious with the domestic paintings of Millais.

The impetus for Lord Leighton's 1892 painting, *And the Sea Gave Up the Dead Which Were in It*, was a proposed scheme to decorate the inner dome of St Paul's Cathedral. The Dean and Chapter of the Cathedral invited Leighton and fellow-RA Sir Edward Poynter to prepare designs for a series of mosaics to adorn the space in 1878. Keren Rosa Hammerschlag writes, in her book on Leighton, "A model of the design was exhibited at the Royal Academy in 1882, and a cartoon was temporarily displayed in St Paul's in 1884. However, due to general pressure against it, a permanent version was never installed."[47] The objections seem to have been technical, rather than aesthetic. The reason for the opposition is suggested by an article in *The Building News and Engineering Journal* for January of 1891, at which point Leighton's and Poynter's proposal had finally been abandoned. The author, having viewed the cartoons for the mosaic panels, wrote, "Although we have no doubt whatever as to the unsuitability of the designs, with their intricate figurework, for the dome of St. Paul's, it is equally certain that" the cartoons "are most interesting, and, beside their intrinsic value, will have historic character more than sufficient at least to justify their proper preservation."[48] *And the Sea* was given new life when the collector Sir Henry Tate commissioned Leighton to paint the picture for his planned National Gallery of British Art.

The final version of Lord Leighton's painting is a monumental work that reflects his mastery of dramatic composition and emotional depth. Inspired by the aforementioned passage from the Book of Revelation, it depicts the apocalyptic resurrection of the dead from the ocean as described in prophecy. The scene is oriented by a diagonal horizon that guides the viewer's eye across the canvas, creating a sense of motion and tension. The sea itself is depicted as a swirling, tempestuous force, with swelling waves and a somber palette of ochre, blue, and gray. Overhead, a radiant light breaks through the darkened sky, symbolizing divine hope amidst the violent upheaval.

The foreground is dominated by three central figures rising out of the water. They are understood to be a family group. The man is fully resurrected, his skin flushed with life, eyes open and elevated toward the unseen source of their miraculous ascension. In his arms he holds his wife and son, pulling them upward with him into the life-giving air. They appear to be in an earlier stage of resurrection. Their skin is still ghostly pale and luminous. The boy clings to his father. His head is nestled as though sleeping, and his legs hang slack, but there is visible tension in the muscle of his arm, revealing the will to life. The woman swoons in her husband's arm, not yet woken. Her head is lolling back. But an arm is raised unconsciously to the fabric of the shroud which has fallen away from her head and breasts. Like a sleeper she is stirring.

Below this central group a single male figure is depicted only just emerging from the waters. His head, shoulders, and chest are visible but everything below is still submerged. He is still dead. His face is not simply pale but mottled with the blues and yellows of decomposition. His eyes are closed. His arms are crossed over his chest and bound in a shroud. And yet his face is tilted to receive the heavenly light from above. The viewer understands that in moments he will become, first like the rousing woman and child, then like the living man.

In the background another resurrected male figure can be seen behind a swell. He is positioned directly under the break of light in the sky at the upper right hand corner. The figure stretches his arms like a man awoken from a long and restful sleep. His coloring, like that of the man in the foreground, is living and healthy. On either side of the canvas coffins have surfaced, floating on the waves. The lids have slid away. The occupants, tightly bound in linens, sit up and look to the sky. One of these sea burials wears the crown of a king. A small portion of the face around the eyes and nose can be seen between the wrappings, still withered and skeletal, but receiving the warmth of divine light with a tender, fragile, almost beatific posture.

In her book on Lord Leighton, subtitled *Death, Mortality, Resurrection*, Keren Rosa Hammerschlag writes that, "In this work, theological discourse on the material resurrection was put in the service of Leighton's artistic project of excavating and reanimating the Classical male body."[49] Conversely, he acted "as theologian, providing his own unique vision of Biblical prophesy" through these forms and poses.[50]

IV. THE DIVINE COMEDY:

Contrasted with these Biblical depictions of Resurrection are the wholly imaginary depictions of an ethereal afterlife that appear most notably in the work of Dante Gabriel Rossetti.

The Blessed Damozel is the title of a poem and a painting by Rossetti. The latter is a visual interpretation of the former. The poem, first published in 1850, and later revised, provides the story. In Rossetti's narrative, the titular Damozel, a woman who has died and ascended in spirit to God's own abode beyond the stars, mourns her separation from a still-living lover. Amidst her heavenly surroundings her heart remains fixed on the earthly beloved. She prays for their reunion, imagining the moment they will meet again in heaven.

Created between 1875 and 1878, the painting depicts the Damozel, leaning out from heaven over a central bar in the actual custom-built frame designed to display the work, gazing longingly toward earth. She is surrounded by a celestial setting, with stars in her hair and a halo of repeating images of her and her lover embracing. Below her, separated by the bar, is a lower panel depicting her lover, lying on his back in the grass by a riverbank, looking up toward her. This division emphasizes the central theme: the separation of lovers by death and the yearning for reunion in the afterlife.

The entire composition, integrating two panels with the frame, is a wonderfully busy endeavor: the Damozel dominates the scene, her flowing hair and intense gaze drawing the viewer in, while the lower panel goes almost unnoticed at first, underscoring her spiritual elevation over the earthly realm. But only once the lower panel is seen does the meaning of the work become clear. Rossetti's symbolism is rich. The golden bar represents the divide between heaven and the earth, life and death. The roses and lilies she holds are classic floral motifs, as elaborated upon in the previous chapter—roses for love, lilies for purity. The lush colors (deep blues, golds, reds) and intricate details—like the texture of her garments—reflect the Pre-Raphaelite attention to beauty and nature. The lover below, often interpreted as a stand-in for Rossetti himself, suggests the artist's personal life, particularly his grief over his late wife. He wrote the poem more than a decade before her death but undertook the painting more than a decade after.

The poem particularly is a kaleidoscope of Christian symbolism and imagery, applied without concern for coherency. At times, Rossetti seems to be describing the New Earth of scripture. The Damozel wishes to lay with her lover in "the shadow of / That living mystic tree / Within whose secret growth the Dove / Sometimes is felt to be".[51] She would seek out "the groves" where Mary dwells among handmaidens, "with bound locks / And bosoms covered".[52] But the setting is not the New Earth. Rossetti explicitly locates the scene on "the terrace of God's house" above "the sheer depth" of the cosmos.[53] Even as this imagery, taken from sacred art, is paraded before the imagination, it is put in service of an uneasy, romantic, personal yearning. The result is a mess of contradictions, from a theological point of view. Properly understood, heaven is God's domain, forever behind a veil, not the location of the human afterlife. The paradise of the New Earth will be opened at once to all resurrected humanity and thus will not be a place where the dead have to wait for the living. Rossetti's heaven functions in the narrative much like his sister's "intermediate state" of expectation and separation.

N.T. Wright blames misconceptions about the Christian afterlife in part on Dante Alighieri's "great poetry, which sets up a Heaven, Purgatory and Hell immediately after death," and which, he argues, "had enormous influence on Western culture, so much so that many Christians think that is Christianity."[54] Certainly Rossetti's depictions of the afterlife owe much to his namesake. The Damozel's celestial abode recalls Dante's *Paradise*. Other, more direct references, can be found throughout his body of work.

Rossetti's father, Gabriele, was an important scholar of medieval Italian literature broadly, and Dante specifically, so it would be natural for the painter to draw upon those influences. But the father was adamant in his insistence that Dante's entire cosmology must not be read literally.

Gabriele Rossetti's 1834 book, *Disquisitions on the Antipapal Spirit*, presents a compelling thesis: that as the Roman Papacy usurped political and ecclesiastical power in Europe during the Middle Ages, an organized opposition movement, sometimes working openly, sometimes in secret, maintained an ongoing defense against the claims of the Pope of Rome, not only giving rise eventually to the Protestant Reformation, but also shaping the literary traditions of Europe. Professor Rossetti argued that this "antipapal spirit" provided a hidden subtext, expressed through coded language and symbolism, in the works of major writers, particularly the Italian vernacular poets like Dante, Petrarch, and Boccaccio.

To this end, the folklorist Thomas Keightley, a friend of the family, scolded the younger Rossetti playfully, in an 1861 letter, "But, you degenerate, you seem to regard the *Vita Nuova* as a real autobiography! Now I not only think but am certain that your father actually demonstrated the contrary. In my mind Beatrice, Laura, Mandetta and all the rest of the bevy are as ideal as Queen Mab."[55] There is no indication that Rossetti ever employed his father's thesis in his own creative interpretation of the Italian *terza rima* poets. But he was certainly using Dante's imagery in a symbolic fashion of his own, not necessarily to be taken literally.

In his book on Rossetti subtitled, *The Limits of Victorian Vision*, David Riede writes that the artist was "not attracted to Christian doctrine or faith" so much as the forms of Christianity. He elaborates that, "just as the Christian reaches to the infinite and eternal God, so the Rossettian lover reaches for some infinite and eternal certainty that, for lack of a better name, he may call God."[56] It is, perhaps, a paradise of eros that Rossetti was attempting to communicate with symbols drawn promiscuously from Christian art.

CHAPTER FIVE
TWILIGHT OF THE GODS

By the final decades of the nineteenth century, the Pre-Raphaelite Brotherhood was no longer a brotherhood at all. The youthful collaboration of its founding members had long since given way to distinct careers shaped by differing temperaments, convictions, and opportunities. And yet, despite—or perhaps because of—its dissolution as an organized movement, Pre-Raphaelitism largely succeeded in its original aims. The artistic principles that had once been dismissed as radical and naïve had become defining features of mainstream British painting and design.

In the early 1870s, Dante Gabriel Rossetti had become one of the most prominent and enigmatic figures in London's artistic life. Since 1862 he was living at 16 Cheyne Walk, the spacious Georgian house, overlooking the Thames, that he had filled with extravagant furnishings, art, bric-a-brac, and wildlife. Rossetti transformed the house into a studio-salon—a space where painting, poetry, and sociability coexisted in an atmosphere of cultivated intensity. It was "a meeting-place for poets and artists during the years 1871–81," an entry in *The*

London Encyclopaedia notes.[1] Rossetti attracted writers and painters, disciples and friends—among them Algernon Charles Swinburne, Ford Madox Brown, William Bell Scott, and James McNeill Whistler. For a time, Rossetti was at the center of a fluid and overlapping circle that linked the last days of Pre-Raphaelitism to the rise of what would later be called the Aesthetic movement. His paintings, with their jewel-like colors and languidly posed figures, dispensed with moral didacticism in favor of an almost hypnotic visual pleasure. This approach resonated with artists like Whistler and Albert Moore, both Aestheticists, whose work suggested Rossetti's own decorative, sensuous style.

In 1870, Rossetti published *Poems*, his first major collection, which included the verses that he had exhumed from Elizabeth Siddal's grave. The book had been anticipated for years, especially among friends who knew of his early sonnets and dramatic monologues. Among the poems were *The House of Life* (then an incomplete sonnet sequence), the monologue *Jenny*, and a handful of religious and historical pieces. Critics divided quickly. Some praised the volume's musicality and imaginative range; others, notably Robert Buchanan, in his essay "The Fleshly School of Poetry," condemned it as morbid and erotic.[2] Though Rossetti received loyal support from Swinburne and others, the episode distressed him. Prone to anxiety, he suffered a collapse in 1872 that was exacerbated by overwork and a growing dependence on chloral hydrate, a sedative.

After this crisis, Rossetti began to withdraw from public life. He no longer attended exhibitions, and though he did not cut himself off entirely from friends, the rhythms of life at Cheyne Walk grew more private. The raucous assemblies of earlier years gave way to smaller gatherings. Among those who stepped into a more central role was Theodore Watts-Dunton, a solicitor-turned-poet and critic, who first entered Rossetti's circle in the early 1870s. He began visiting more frequently, eventually taking rooms in the house. Practical, discreet, and devoted, Watts-Dunton helped manage Rossetti's affairs, encouraged regular meals, and attempted to limit access to more disruptive visitors. The household also included Rossetti's longtime assistant Henry Treffry Dunn, his family, servants, and a few regular callers. Among the newer arrivals was Hall Caine, a young admirer from the Isle of Man, who visited for the first time in 1880 and soon became his secretary. Caine went on to become a bestselling novelist and playwright.

Though quieter, Rossetti's life in these years was still devoted to his artistic activities. He continued to paint, often revisiting earlier subjects or reworking unfinished compositions. *Dante's Dream*, one of his most ambitious works, remained in his studio, undergoing intermittent revision. Other canvases—*The Blessed Damozel*, *La Bella Mano*, *The Day Dream*—were returned to, sometimes to fulfill commissions, sometimes in search of better realization. His models included Alexa Wilding and Jane Morris, whose faces appeared again and again in different guises. *Astarte Syriaca* was the last painting for which Jane Morris sat, in 1875, at the end of their relationship, though her likeness continued to appear on Rossetti's canvas. *The Day Dream*, completed in 1880, depicts Jane in a pensive reverie amidst a greenwood. Though his physical energy was limited, Rossetti remained methodical and absorbed in his work when he was able to paint.

He never forgot Lizzie. The American writer Elbert Hubbard tells a story of Effie Millais visiting Cheyne Walk in 1870. When she had the "occasion to hang her wraps in a wardrobe," she noticed "the dresses that had once belonged to Mrs. Rossetti hanging from the same hooks" as his clothes.

Apologetically, Rossetti told her, "You see, if I did not find traces of her all over the house I should surely die."[3]

During this period, he returned to poetry. He had continued to revise and expand *The House of Life*, seeking to complete it as a unified sequence. In the later 1870s, he also began composing new narrative ballads and sonnets. With the help of Watts-Dunton and Caine, he prepared a second volume, *Ballads and Sonnets*, which was published in 1881. The book contained the completed *House of Life*, along with *The White Ship*, *Rose Mary*, and *Soothsay*, among others. The poems were dense, symbolic, and written in an ornate style that echoed — and in places exceeded — the register of his earlier work. The volume received a more favorable response than *Poems*, and Rossetti took quiet satisfaction in its publication. It would be the last book issued during his lifetime.

Rossetti's health had grown worse. He was suffering from advanced Bright's disease; his kidneys were failing. Moreover, a case of the mumps years earlier had left him with chronic hydrocele, an accumulation of fluid around the testicles, that caused swelling. His use of chloral persisted, though under some supervision. Visitors to Cheyne Walk described him as alternately lucid and withdrawn, depending on the day. He continued to make minor adjustments to canvases and occasionally dictated letters, but by 1881 it was clear that he required a change of atmosphere. In early 1882, on Watts-Dunton's advice, Rossetti left London for Birchington-on-Sea, a small coastal village in Kent, where he rented a house.

During his final weeks at Birchington, Rossetti was mostly bedridden. Nevertheless, he received family and friends. His brother found him frail but alert, still editing poetry and organizing commissions. His sister Christina read diverting novels to him: *Dead Secret* by Wilkie Collins, *Dead Men's Shoes* by Mary Elizabeth Braddon, *A Tale of Two Cities* by Charles Dickens.[4]

The last creative work that Rossetti undertook was a poem in two sonnets intended to accompany a drawing of *The Sphinx* he had made years earlier. "Ah, when those everlasting lips unlock," he wrote, "And the old riddle of the world is read, what shall man find? or seeks he evermore?"[5]

Rossetti died at Birchington on Easter Sunday, April 9, 1882, at the age of 53. He was buried at All Saints Church in Birchington. Watts-Dunton handled the arrangements, and the funeral was attended by a small group of mourners. Reports of his death appeared in the London newspapers over the following days.[6]

While Rossetti's final years were shaped by retreat, John Everett Millais moved in the opposite direction: into public life, institutional acclaim, and growing national visibility. By the start of the 1870s, Millais had become an established and financially successful painter, no longer associated with the radicalism of the Brotherhood's early years. He had married Effie Gray in 1855, and they now had eight children. Domestic life, social obligations, and the expectations of clients increasingly shaped the trajectory of his career. What had once been a crusade for artistic truth had, by degrees, become a career of refinement, discipline, and public service.

Millais had begun to move away from Pre-Raphaelitism in the late 1850s, favoring a broader and more painterly style. By the 1870s, he was one of the most popular and sought-after commissioned artists in Britain. His technical mastery remained undiminished, but his subjects shifted to landscapes and genre pictures, then portraits. His facility with likeness, his ease with fashionable settings, and his confident speed of work made him a natural choice for society portraiture. He painted politicians, writers, actresses, aristocrats, and children. These commissions brought prestige and steady income, and by the end of the decade they had become his principal occupation.

Among his narrative works from this period was *The North-West Passage* (1874), a painting of an elderly sea captain poring over maps, accompanied by his daughter. The subject was fictional, but the theme—courage, perseverance, British character—resonated with contemporary audiences. It was shown at the Royal Academy and widely reproduced. Other pictures from the 1870s and 1880s, such as *The Boyhood of Raleigh* and *The Princes in the Tower*, likewise combined historical or patriotic subjects with a polished narrative style.

Millais also turned to sentimental genre scenes, particularly of children. *My First Sermon* (1863) and *My Second Sermon* (1864), had already proven popular with the public. In both, a young girl sits in a church pew — attentive in the first canvas, drowsy in the second — dressed in bright red against a subdued background. These images, at once tender and gently humorous, were widely reproduced as engravings and established a precedent for similarly sentimental treatments. In the 1880s, Millais returned to this theme with *Cherry Ripe* (1879), a painting of a young girl seated on a log, cherries beside her, looking out at the viewer with solemn poise. Inspired by Joshua Reynolds's *Penelope Boothby*, the painting was commissioned by *The Graphic* newspaper and became a sensation. The model, Edie Ramage, was the editor's niece. The image became enormously popular, reappearing in countless prints and reproductions.

The most well known of these later works, though perhaps the artist would have preferred otherwise, was *Bubbles* (1886), painted from a study of Millais's grandson, William James. Officially titled *A Child's World*, it depicted the boy blowing a soap bubble—a classic *memento mori* motif. The transience of the bubble represents the transience of life floating before the child's eye. Rendered with exceptional delicacy, the image resonated with Victorian sensibilities. It attracted the attention of the Pears Soap company, which purchased the repro-duction rights from Millais's dealer, Thomas Agnew & Sons. Without Millais's direct involvement, *Bubbles* became the centerpiece of an advertisement campaign. The image—with a bar of soap added, of course—became ubiquitous. While it secured financial rewards, the commercial use of the painting drew criticism. Millais was accused of compromising his artistic dignity. Millais defended the decision by noting that the reproduction rights, once sold, were no longer under his control. Millais's grandson, Admiral Sir William Milbourne James, would be known by the nickname "Bubbles" throughout his life.

During these years, Millais worked at a steady and at times relentless pace. With a large household to support and constant demand for new work, he accepted portrait commis-sions in great number. His sitters included William Gladstone and Benjamin Disraeli, Lord Tennyson, Thomas Carlyle, Wilkie Collins, and many others. When Thomas Carlyle visited Millais's residence at No. 2 Palace Gate, Kensington, in 1877, to sit for his portrait, he remarked on the grand interior, "Millais, did painting do all that? Well, there must be more fools in this world than I had thought!"[7] His portraits were noteworthy for their psychological immediacy and painterly confidence. They were often painted rapidly—some in just a few sittings—and many were engraved and widely distributed. Millais's studio had become a required stop for the distinguished and ambitious.

In the autumn, Millais would leave London on excursions to his wife's native Scotland where he would paint *en plein air*, yielding brooding landscapes like *The Sound of Many Waters (1876)*, *The Old Garden* (1883), and *Dew-drenched Furze* (1890), that dispensed with symbolism in favor of mood, weather, and texture. These landscapes, while often melancholic in tone, displayed a mastery of natural atmosphere and an intuitive sense of light. His mature style, freer and less precise than his Pre-Raphaelite work, was admired by younger artists, including Vincent van Gogh, who praised Millais's ability to capture the feeling of place.[8]

Millais's *entrée* into the establishment was confirmed by a series of late-life honors. In 1885, he was created a baronet. He was the first British artist to receive a hereditary title. In 1896, shortly before his death, Millais was elected President of the Royal Academy, succeeding Lord Leighton. In his final years, Millais had developed a cancer of the throat that made speaking and swallowing difficult. He continued to work through the illness. Millais died on August 13, 1896, at the age of sixty-seven. He was buried in St. Paul's Cathedral, among the kingdom's heroes.

Millais's death left William Holman Hunt as the last of the original Pre-Raphaelite artists. Unlike Millais, who had embraced public sentiment and institutional favor, Hunt remained committed throughout his life to the symbolic and religious aims that had defined his earliest work.

In 1875, William Holman Hunt returned to Jerusalem, accompanied by his second wife, Edith, and his young son Cyril. The family settled into a house Hunt had built on the Street of the Prophets, a broad new thoroughfare just outside the Old City walls. He had long regarded the Holy Land as essential to his religious imagination, and his sojourns there were motivated by a kind of spiritual fidelity to truth in art. Hunt continued an ongoing project to observe, study, and absorb the local landscape and customs begun decades earlier. This project had informed the ethnographic accuracy of the figures in his picture, *The Finding of the Saviour in the Temple*, painted during his first stay in the city. His studies from the period record architectural details, faces and fabrics, as well as the iridescent moonlight over the Mediterranean. In 1876, Edith gave birth to their daughter, Gladys, during the family's residency in Jerusalem. They remained abroad for several years, returning to England in 1878, shortly before the birth of their son, Hilary.

Hunt had by now stopped exhibiting at the Royal Academy, preferring the more sympathetic Grosvenor Gallery or the New Gallery. He viewed the Academy as inhospitable to symbolic art. In the mid-1880s, he supported a group of reformers who criticized the Academy's exclusivity and helped organize exhibitions that presented fine and decorative art together—efforts broadly aligned with, though distinct from, the Arts and Crafts movement. During this period Hunt began work on *The Lady of Shalott*. It would be a grand and complex illustration of Lord Tennyson's Arthurian poem.

A major retrospective of Hunt's work was mounted at the Fine Arts Society in 1886, offering the public a comprehensive view of his career to date. It brought renewed attention to his early Pre-Raphaelite paintings and prompted critical reflection on his role in the formation of a symbolic, religiously oriented genre.

During the last decade of his life, Hunt's vision deteriorated from glaucoma. By the late 1890s, he was unable to continue painting in the same way he had in earlier years. He enlisted the skills of an assistant, Edward Robert Hughes, who helped him with the final stages of his paintings, ensuring that Hunt's "vision" remained intact despite his failing eyesight. In the early 1900s, with Hughes's help, Hunt completed a large-scale version of a design he had originally executed in the 1850s.

Hunt painted his famous work of Christian allegory, *The Light of the World*, in three versions between 1851 and 1904. This final version was installed at St Paul's Cathedral in

London after a triumphant tour of the Commonwealth. The original hangs in a side chapel of Keble College, Oxford. Ayla Lepine, writing in *The Oxford History of Anglicanism*, describes it as marking "the establishment of an Anglican aesthetic," in the latter years of the gothic revival.[9] *The Light of the World* portrays Christ knocking on the door of a house at the end of the night. He holds a lantern at his side, casting a warm subtle glow over the foreground, where a garden has been given over to weeds and vines. It is an illustration of the words from Revelation 3:20, "Behold, I stand at the door, and knock: if any man hear my voice, and open the door, I will come in to him, and will sup with him, and he with me." The overgrown garden corresponds to the neglected state of the human soul, which is in need of renewal.

In 1905, Hunt published *Pre-Raphaelitism and the Pre-Raphaelite Brotherhood*, a two-volume memoir documenting the founding of the movement and his own lifelong artistic principles. Together with John Guille Millais's collection of his father's writing, and William Michael Rossetti's various memoirs, it is the foundational primary source for the history of the movement. Hunt used the book to correct public misconceptions, defend the Brotherhood's early ideals, and define his own legacy. Woven throughout are Hunt's reflections on the ethical and, at times, religious implications of art — themes that were central to his view of the artist's responsibility. Hunt's religious convictions were grounded in a devout and intellectually engaged Evangelical Protestantism: scriptural, moral, and serious in tone, but resistant to ritualism or theological abstraction. His faith informed both the subjects he chose and the symbolic detail he insisted upon.

The same year that his memoir was published, Hunt was awarded the Order of Merit by King Edward VII, and received an honorary Doctor of Civil Law degree from the University of

Oxford. In 1907, on his eightieth birthday, friends and admirers presented his painting *The Ship* to the Tate Gallery as a commemorative gift. Hunt was increasingly infirm by this time, and the presentation served as a gesture of esteem and affection at the close of a long career.

He spent his final years quietly in London, living with his family at 18 Melbury Road in Kensington. Though nearly blind, he remained mentally sharp and continued to correspond with former colleagues, patrons, and younger artists. When weather permitted, he visited his country retreat in Sonning-on-Thames.

Hunt died on September 7, 1910, at the age of eighty-three. His funeral was held at St Paul's Cathedral, where he was interred near Millais. The two had remained lifelong friends. Before Hunt first departed for the Holy Land in 1854, Millais, overwhelmed at the thought of their parting, had asked him to purchase a signet ring and wear it always, as a token of their friendship. Hunt commissioned the ring from Hunt and Roskell, the London jewelers, and had it engraved with his own initials, "WHH," interposed with Millais's initial "M."[10] He wore it for the rest of his life.

CHAPTER SIX

THE WHEEL OF FORTUNE

One day in 1962, a teenage Andrew Lloyd Webber paused outside a framer's shop on the King's Road in London to look at a painting in the window. It was *Flaming June*, a luminous portrait by Lord Leighton, of a woman cloaked in folds of brilliant orange, sleeping on a marble bench, beneath a haze of Mediterranean light. Once praised as a masterpiece of late Victorian art, the painting had somehow found its way into obscurity, offered for the trivial sum of fifty pounds. Lloyd Webber returned home to ask his grandmother if she would lend him the money to purchase it. Her reply was swift and final: "I will not have that Victorian junk in my flat."[1]

This anecdote captures something of the mid-twentieth-century fate of Victorian art. Within a few decades of their deaths, painters who had once enjoyed popularity and institutional support had quietly slipped from view. Artists like Leighton, Alma-Tadema, and the Pre-Raphaelites were no longer central to the culture; their work had become associated with a bygone era. To many mid-century eyes, these paintings seemed curiously remote—technically impressive, certainly, but out of step with prevailing fashions. Modernism had redefined the philosophy and priorities of the art world.

This chapter explores the arc of that decline—and the remarkable revival that followed. It begins with the question of how, and why, the artists fell so thoroughly out of favor during the early twentieth century, charting the rise of abstraction, the rejection of figurative idealism, and the cultural recasting of "Victorian" as a byword for repression and excess. But the story does not end in oblivion. Through the rediscovery of Victorian forms by a younger generation, and the work of collectors, scholars, critics, and dealers, the second half of the twentieth century witnessed a decisive reappraisal. By the time of the landmark 1984 Tate Gallery exhibition that signaled their reestablishment, the Pre-Raphaelites were not merely back in fashion—they had been restored to a permanent place in the British canon.

At the close of the nineteenth century, Victorian artists enjoyed a public profile that might have seemed unassailable. The influence of the Pre-Raphaelites had extended far beyond the confines of painting. Their approach—rooted in craftsmanship, historical romanticism, and symbolism—radiated outward into the decorative arts, shaping everything from book design and stained glass to textiles, ceramics, and interior decoration. Through disciples like William Morris and Edward Burne-Jones, their aesthetic ideals helped define the Arts and Crafts movement and filtered into the visual language of everyday life. In Britain and abroad, these ideas spread into illustration and popular media. In the United States, artists like Howard Pyle and N.C. Wyeth—known for their romantic literary scenes—echoed the Pre-Raphaelites' emphasis on narrative, nature, and moral idealism. After the artists themselves were gone, their sensibility lingered in the public imagination, exerting tremendous influence over the look and feel of turn-of-the-century culture.

Even before World War I there were signs of change. The American actress Elsie de Wolfe, later known by her married title, Lady Mendl, was a leading figure in the transformation of interior design. De Wolfe had grown up surrounded by the dark woodwork, heavy upholstery, and densely layered ornamentation of a typical Victorian home. She came to view such spaces as antithetical to comfort, clarity, and modern life. Her style, developed in the early years of the twentieth century, favored pale walls, light fabrics, painted furniture, and an overall atmosphere of airiness and order. She advocated for a radical simplification of domestic space, writing in her 1913 book, *The House in Good Taste*, "I believe in plenty of optimism and white paint."[2] This phrase was a shorthand for her philosophy: one that rejected the richness and *mélange* of nineteenth century design in favor of openness, light, and a sense of ease. De Wolfe's interiors, widely published and emulated, helped shape a new ideal of domestic taste—one in which Victorian design was not only considered outmoded but actively oppressive.

The early decades of the twentieth century saw the steady rise of Modernism, a broad artistic movement that favored subjectivity, innovation, abstraction, and formal experimentation. The values at the heart of Victorian painting came under increasing scrutiny. Paintings were no longer judged by their narrative coherence or technical finish but by their ability to provoke, to challenge, or to distill emotion into abstract form.

This transformation was partly aesthetic, but it also reflected a broader philosophical shift in critical opinion and institutional taste after the First World War. For the ascendant cultural establishment, the moral confidence and visual romanticism of an earlier generation was regarded as being out of touch. In light of the collapse of empires and the mecha-nized brutality of twentieth-century warfare, the moral certainties of Victorian art were dismissed as naïve and irrele-vant. By the interwar period, Victorian painting had become associated with a kind of ornamental conservatism. The word "Victorian" itself was undergoing a semantic shift—it no longer referred only to the historical period, but to a set of perceived attitudes: moralism, sentimentality, excess. The arti-facts of the nineteenth century were treated, at best, as nostalgic curiosities.

Popular culture, too, reflected this reassessment. The mystery novelist Agatha Christie made reference to Victorian art, as a dividing line between generations, in her Miss Marple series. The central character is a shrewd amateur detective in the person of an elderly spinster. In the 1964 novel, *A Caribbean Mystery*, the reader is told that Miss Marple's nephew, Raymond, is "[a]lways trying to bring her up to date. Sending her books to read. Modern novels. So difficult—all about such unpleasant people, doing such very odd things and not, appar-ently, even enjoying them."[3] In "Miss Marple Tells a Story," a work of short fiction published in 1934, the title character remarks to her nephew, "I am hopelessly Victorian. I admire Mr Alma-Tadema and Mr Frederick Leighton, and I suppose to you they are hopelessly *vieux jeu*."[4] The line is brief but telling. The French expression means "old fashioned," literally, "old game" in English. Miss Marple's admission is offered with a hint of wry self-awareness. Kirsty Stonell Walker writes, in an essay on the subject, that "Miss Marple is the archetypal maiden aunt, born around the 1870s (as she appears to be a woman of 50-60 in her first appearance in 1927, and grows older up to the 1950s)." The character is conceding that she, too, may be *vieux jeu*, of course. But Christie was also defending what must have been a large segment of the population in the first half of the twentieth century who thought highly of Victorian art, and whose position was largely ignored. Walker writes, "When Miss Marple says how 'old fashioned' her tastes are in comparison to her nephew's sordid books" or his wife's "paintings of lumpy people and sad vases, Christie is obviously having a cheeky dig at modern tastes. More than that though, by making Miss Marple favour Victorian art" she is identifying the genre with "high intelligence, common sense and goodness" because Miss Marple "might be hopelessly *vieux jeu* but she's never wrong."[5]

The passing of the Victorian generation accelerated this trend. By the 1940s and 1950s, it was possible for a British museum visitor to walk through galleries with little sense of the prominence that nineteenth century art had once enjoyed. Curators re-hung their permanent collections to emphasize more recent developments in Modernism.

Tim Barringer, writing in the *Journal of Victorian Culture*, credits "a mood of anti-Victorian self-hatred among British institutions," for the decision of the Victoria and Albert Museum to obscure "the magnificent decorations of the South Court," in 1949, "including frescoes by Frederic Leighton, filling in Francis Fowke's elegant arcades with a shoddy asbestos-ridden white cube."[6] The Tate Gallery, then the National Gallery of British Art, was founded in 1897 largely on Sir Henry Tate's donation of Victorian paintings. Yet by the mid-20th century the Tate's curators were giving those very works low priority. In the 1950s and early 1960s, Victorian art was so out of favor that the Tate consigned its Pre-Raphaelite collection to a small room in the basement—infamously next to the public lavatories—rather than prominent galleries.[7] This was a deliberate curatorial strategy reflecting the institution's mission to collect contemporary art. In 1966, the Tate hosted a retrospective of the French surrealist Marcel

Duchamp, including his notorious piece, *Fountain*, which consists entirely of a ready-made porcelain urinal, signed, "R. Mutt."

It was during this same decade that *Flaming June* ended up in the framer's shop window. The story of how it got there may be apocryphal. Originally purchased by *The Graphic* magazine, which intended to reproduce it, the painting was hung in the window of the editorial offices overlooking The Strand to be visible as Leighton's funeral procession passed by in 1896. Around the turn of the century, it was loaned to the Ashmolean Museum in Oxford, but by the 1930s it had disappeared from public view and public record.[8] According to an oft-repeated account, *Flaming June* was rediscovered in 1962 by a builder, concealed behind a panel above a chimney-piece in a house he was renovating or demolishing. Perhaps it had been boarded up for protection during the Blitz and forgotten about. It was ultimately acquired by the Puerto Rican industrialist Luis A. Ferré and became a centerpiece of the Museo de Arte de Ponce in Puerto Rico, where it remains.

Even as Victorian painting fell out of fashion, it survived—not because it was universally admired, but because it had already been institutionalized. The foresight (or good taste) of nineteenth-century collectors, and the infrastructure of public museums that had grown up around their gifts, created a framework of preservation. Without these centralized holdings, the art might not have weathered the long decades of neglect.

The earliest of these benefactors was John Sheepshanks, a Yorkshire textile manufacturer and advocate for British art. In 1857, he donated his collection of over two hundred paintings to what would become the South Kensington Museum—later the Victoria and Albert Museum—insisting they remain free to the public in perpetuity. He assembled a representative body of mid-Victorian painting, including works by J.M.W. Turner, John Constable, and Edwin Landseer, along with examples of narrative genre painting then at the height of popularity. A generation later, Sir Henry Tate, the sugar magnate and philanthropist, would donate his own collection of British art—much of it Victorian, including several key Pre-Raphaelite works—to the newly established National Gallery of British Art in 1897. That institution was founded in large part around his bequest. The continuity of the collection ensured that the Pre-Raphaelites, even in periods of neglect, remained in care. A few years after Tate's gift, Constantine Ionides, a London stockbroker and collector, bequeathed his more eclectic and progressive collection to the South Kensington Museum in 1900. His tastes leaned toward the aesthetic and the avant-garde, and his bequest included works by Rossetti, Burne-Jones, Whistler, and other associated artists. Together, these three men and others like them created an institutional foundation for British nineteenth-century painting that would quietly outlast the changing fashions of the twentieth.

Similar patterns played out elsewhere. In Liverpool, George Rae, a wealthy banker and early patron of Dante Gabriel Rossetti, assembled a formidable collection that later shaped the holdings of the Walker Art Gallery. In the northwest of England, William Lever, 1st Viscount Leverhulme, acquired a trove of Victorian paintings as part of his vision for what would become the Lady Lever Art Gallery in Port Sunlight. These collections, often shaped by personal enthusiasm and untroubled by changing academic taste, became sanctuaries of a kind —repositories for a now-unfashionable aesthetic that would be vindicated by future generations. In Birmingham, a combination of municipal ambition and regional pride drove the city to acquire significant works by Burne-Jones, Holman Hunt, and Ford Madox Brown—many of them purchased directly from the artists or their studios. Burne-Jones was a native of Birmingham. These regional collections were arguably more stable than their London counterparts. Civic museums had neither the financial pressure nor the critical spotlight that led some national institutions to rotate or sideline their Victorian holdings.

Afterward, the very inertia of museums worked in the paintings' favor. Once acquired—especially through bequests—they were rarely sold or deaccessioned. The Victoria and Albert Museum, despite closing its dedicated picture galleries after the Second World War, and converting them to display metalwork and arms, kept both the Sheepshanks and Ionides collections intact. The Tate Gallery, though it increasingly emphasized modern and contemporary art in its main displays, never disposed of the Victorian works it had inherited, even if it relegated them to less-frequented galleries. The art remained, if not in place of honor, at least accessible.

Outside Britain, too, there were connoisseurs who built important collections. In the United States, Samuel Bancroft Jr., a textile magnate from Delaware, began collecting Pre-Raphaelite art in the 1890s and eventually built the largest such collection outside of the United Kingdom. His acquisitions—many bought directly from surviving members of the circle—now form the heart of the Delaware Art Museum.

By the early 1960s, the reputation of Victorian painting had reached its lowest ebb. Yet even then, there were signs that the tide was beginning to turn. A new generation of collectors, dealers, and scholars began to look again at the works their predecessors had dismissed. What they found was an entire body of art that had been left out of the modern narrative: technically accomplished, intellectually ambitious, and deeply rooted in its own cultural moment. The long interlude of critical neglect had, in a way, cleared the stage.

No one played a more decisive role in the revival of Victorian painting than the London dealer Jeremy Maas, who almost single-handedly created a market where none had existed. In December of 1960, with more conviction than capital, he opened the Maas Gallery at No. 15a Clifford Street in London.[9] The following year, just before Christmas, he staged *The Pre-Raphaelites and Their Contemporaries*, the first commercial exhibition devoted to the Pre-Raphaelites in the twentieth century. At the time, Victorian painting, particularly narrative or symbolic work, was so far out of favor that few dealers even attempted to sell it. Landscapes from the early nineteenth century dominated the market; works of moral, religious, or esoteric content were largely absent.

His breakthrough exhibition brought together more than a hundred works on paper and a small group of paintings, many of them drawn from private hands or descendants of the artists themselves. The roster included not only Rossetti, Burne-Jones, Millais, Holman Hunt, and Ford Madox Brown, but also lesser-known artists such as Edward Hughes, Frederick Sandys, Simeon Solomon, and William Bell Scott. Among the lenders were descendants of the Pre-Raphaelites like Diana Holman-Hunt, granddaughter of the artist, and Helen Rossetti Angeli, daughter of William, who provided works by both Dante Gabriel Rossetti and Elizabeth Siddal. For many, it was their first opportunity to see this material presented with curatorial seriousness and coherence.

The response was enthusiastic. A second exhibition followed the next year, and over time the gallery developed a reputation as a meeting place for scholars, collectors, and museum professionals. Maas's success lay not only in his eye but in his tremendous interest in the broad range of Victorian culture. He read widely—memoirs, exhibition reviews, letters, and early art criticism—amassing a vast archive of nineteenth-century sources. His gallery became an unofficial center for Victorian studies, a place where knowledge and commerce intersected. He published several books, including *Victorian Painters* (1969), which became a foundational reference, and *Gambart: Prince of the Victorian Art World* (1975), a biography of the nineteenth-century art dealer. He was also an accomplished discoverer of lost or misattributed works. He tracked down Waterhouse's *St Cecilia* in a private home in France and handled important pieces by Dyce, Tissot, and Rossetti. Most famously, it was Maas who acquired *Flaming June* in 1963, placing it with Ferré, after failing to persuade any British institution to take it on.

The 1960s also produced a new generation of museum curators with an interest in Victorian painting. One of the most important was Mary Bennett, curator of the Walker Art Gallery in Liverpool, who staged a series of exhibitions that would prove pivotal. In 1964, the Walker mounted a major retrospective of Ford Madox Brown, followed in 1967 by a show dedicated to John Everett Millais, and in 1969 by a retrospective of William Holman Hunt. These exhibitions attracted press attention, public interest, and scholarly engagement. By the early 1970s, interest was sufficient that Christie's launched dedicated auctions of Victorian material.

By the start of the 1970s, the long marginalization of Victorian painting was beginning to reverse in earnest. What had once been the preserve of collectors and connoisseurs was now drawing the attention of museums, publishers, and a wider public. Scholars who had previously ignored the period began to reassess its critical and cultural significance. Prices at auction rose sharply, Victorian subjects reappeared on book covers and posters, and a new generation of viewers encountered these works on their own terms. After decades in the wilderness, the Victorians were returning to view.

Regional museums had led the way in the 1960s, but by the 1970s national institutions were beginning to follow suit. In 1970, the Royal Academy mounted *The Victorian Revival*, an ambitious survey that drew together painting, sculpture, architecture, and decorative arts from across the nineteenth century. Two years later, the Tate Gallery mounted a major retrospective of Edward Burne-Jones. The exhibition was a success. These were turning points that demonstrated a public appetite for the art of the period, and helped shift institutional priorities. The momentum was sustained throughout the decade. In 1974, the Victoria and Albert exhibited Holman Hunt's *The Light of the World* in its newly restored frame. In 1975, the Metropolitan Museum of Art in New York hosted *The Pre-Raphaelite Legacy*, one of the first major American exhibitions devoted to the movement, organized in collaboration with the Delaware Art Museum.

The revival of interest in Victorian painting reached its culmination in the spring of 1984, when the Tate Gallery mounted a major exhibition devoted to the Pre-Raphaelite Brotherhood and its circle. Simply titled *The Pre-Raphaelites*, the show opened in June to enormous public attention. It was, by any measure, a landmark event: the first time Britain's premier modern art institution had devoted such a scale of resources, gallery space, and publicity to these artists in more than half a century. What began in the 1960s as a dealer-led rediscovery had become, two decades later, an official act of cultural rehabilitation.

Curated by Alan Bowness and Leslie Parris, the 1984 exhibition was ambitious in scope. It brought together over 180 works, drawn from public and private collections in Britain, the United States, and Europe, many of which had not been seen together since the nineteenth century. Paintings by Millais, Rossetti, Holman Hunt, Ford Madox Brown, and

Burne-Jones were shown alongside preparatory drawings, letters, illustrated books, and decorative designs. The exhibition presented the Pre-Raphaelites as a coherent, innovative, and intellectual movement—one that had meaningfully shaped the trajectory of British art. The response was overwhelming. Attendance figures were estimated at well over two hundred thousand visitors for the duration of the show's run.[10]

The Pre-Raphaelite revival seemed finally to have achieved escape velocity. New exhibitions followed: *The Last Romantics* at the Barbican in 1989 traced the later legacies of Pre-Raphaelitism into the early twentieth century. In 1998, *Edward Burne-Jones: Victorian Artist-Dreamer* opened at the Metropolitan Museum of Art before traveling to the Birmingham Museum and the Musée d'Orsay in Paris. *Holman Hunt and the Pre-Raphaelite Vision* followed in 2008 at Manchester Art Gallery, gathering over fifty key works. The next year, *J.W. Waterhouse: The Modern Pre-Raphaelite* went on tour at the Groninger Museum in the Netherlands to the Royal Academy of Arts in London and finally to Montreal.

In 2012, The Tate mounted a second major exhibition devoted to the movement: *Pre-Raphaelites: Victorian Avant-Garde*. Where the 1984 retrospective had focused on reestablishing the Pre-Raphaelites within the canon of British art, the 2012 exhibition aimed to position them more boldly—as innovators, even radicals. Curators Tim Barringer, Jason Rosenfeld, and Alison Smith framed the group as a self-conscious avant-garde: artists who rejected academic convention, challenged artistic hierarchies, and explored the social conditions of modern life.

For much of the twentieth century, the Tate Gallery had operated as both a museum of historic British paintings and the principle venue for modern and contemporary art. This changed with the opening of the Tate Modern in 2000, which enabled a more balanced division of resources between its different collections. Modern and contemporary works were moved across the Thames to new galleries at the former Bankside Power Station in Southwark, while the original Millbank building was rebranded as Tate Britain, devoted primarily to the historic collection. Today the original Victorian acquisitions around which the Tate had been built occupy the central galleries.

The renewal of Victorian art was also shaped by the evolving presentation of the nineteenth century at the Victoria and Albert Museum. In the early 2000s, a project to restore the South Court to its original design was announced, "literally removing the white cube," as Barringer puts it.[11] Throughout the galleries, painting and sculpture are displayed in context of the wider visual and material culture of the era: furniture, textiles, ceramics, stained glass, fashion. The museum's own ironwork, mosaics, terracotta façades, and richly ornamented interiors form part of that presentation. Many of the original galleries retain their proportions and decorative schemes, creating an architectural frame that compliments the objects on display.

This continuity between setting and subject finds its most eloquent expression in the museum's refreshment rooms, widely recognized as the world's first museum café. Designed in the 1860s under the supervision of founding director Henry Cole, the café was conceived as an extension of the museum's educational mission: a space where the public would be surrounded by good design. Three adjoining rooms survive from the original scheme, each a masterwork of Victorian decorative arts. The Morris Room, originally the Green Dining Room, was designed by William Morris, Edward Burne-Jones, and Philip Webb. It remains an exemplary architectural expression of the Pre-Raphaelite aesthetic: dark wood panelling in an Elizabethan style, topped by green plaster walls decorated with a pattern of olive branches, and stained glass windows. It is a space that brings the movement's ideals into practical experience—where the beauty of daily life, the unity of the arts, and the moral dignity of labour are rendered into the atmosphere.

The revival of Victorian art is no longer provisional. The culture of the nineteenth century has become a touchstone of the popular historic imagination. British television played no small role in these developments. Beginning with the original series *Upstairs, Downstairs* in 1971, and followed by adaptations of Victorian literature, produced throughout the 1970s and 1980s, the Victorian world has been "brought to life" for mass audiences with remarkable consistency. Viewers who encountered the period through drawing-room dramas or serialized films of novels and plays came to it not as distant history but as a living world: immersive and aesthetically engaging.

As the most popular storytelling medium of its time, television created a point of intersection that encouraged renewed interest across other media. Hugh Greene's *The Rivals of Sherlock Holmes*—a series of book anthologies dedicated to Victorian detective fiction—was adapted into a television series in the early 1970s, helping to inspire a sustained appetite for period mysteries on screen and in print. This cross-pollination of publishing, broadcasting, and heritage interest created a fertile environment for Victorian culture to reenter the mainstream. Even the Pre-Raphaelite Brotherhood became the subject of a television drama: *The Love School*, broadcast by the BBC in 1975, which portrayed the romantic and artistic passions of Rossetti, Millais, and Holman Hunt with production design evocative of the painters' own style.[12]

CHAPTER SEVEN

RETROSPECTIVE

Today the Victorian period occupies a special place in our popular culture. Every year it is recreated on page, stage, and screen in pastiche. No other era is revisited with such regularity. What is it that fascinates us? Was a different modernity possible? Something more romantic? Something more authentic? A future of dirigibles, post offices, electromagnetism, Prussian monarchy on the Continent, railways instead of motorways, heritage crafts, classical education, art and architecture that continued to develop within the Western vernacular not against it? I believe we see in the Victorian past a future that might have been. *Or that might yet be.* The Victorians were forced by the exigencies of history to find a balance between tradition and innovation—hierarchy and populism—community and individuality—the old and the new. These forces coexisted, if not always comfortably, then effectively. We have lost that balance. Sooner or later the exigencies of our own history may demand that we strike it again.

In revisiting Victorian art, we are not only looking backward. We are testing the idea that beauty and progress might once have belonged to the same project. It is a seemingly uncontroversial idea that nevertheless challenges our assumptions about what it means to be modern.

Among the artists of the nineteenth century, none embodied the tension between tradition and innovation more poignantly than the Pre-Raphaelites. In their search for authenticity, they drew subjects and techniques from the past. Yet their paintings were highly attuned to modern concerns about sex, nature, industry, religion, and the estrangement of beauty from utility.

Over the course of this book, we have followed their journey: from the initial shock of their debut to the eventual absorption of their ideals into the broader Victorian cultural fabric. We have examined their subjects, their techniques, and the imaginative worlds they created—worlds steeped in nature, poetry, and spiritual yearning. From their earliest efforts to reform British art, these painters pursued a vocabulary of intensity. Their scenes are saturated with color, detail, and mood—evoking a sense of luminous strangeness, intense feeling, and private myth. They speak in a visual language that is timeless. The Pre-Raphaelites believed that beauty could be radical, that imagination could be precise, that art could communicate with the clarity of vision, and the mystery of dream.

For those who wish to trace the lives of the Pre-Raphaelites in London, the city still holds their memories. In Bloomsbury, the house where the Brotherhood was founded—7 Gower Street—remains standing, marked by a blue plaque. Along the Thames in Chelsea, Rossetti's old house at 16 Cheyne Walk is likewise commemorated—as are the redbrick façades of 2 Palace Gate, where Millais spent his later years, and 18 Melbury Road, the last house of Holman Hunt, both in Kensington. All of these are private residences today, visible only from the street. A short walk away in Holland Park, however, Leighton House survives as a museum; its domed Arab Hall and vast, light-filled studio preserve something of the splendor and exoticism of the artist's world.

The works themselves can be found throughout the city's collections: at the Tate Britain, Millais's *Ophelia*, Rossetti's *Proserpine*, and Holman Hunt's *The Awakening Conscience*, among so many others; at the Guildhall Art Gallery, Rossetti's *La Ghirlandata*; at the National Portrait Gallery, Millais's paintings of Prime Ministers; at St Paul's Cathedral, the most famous version of Hunt's *The Light of the World*.

London is also the burial place of many Pre-Raphaelite figures. Millais, Hunt, and Leighton are interred in the crypt of St Paul's. Rossetti, by contrast, was buried in Kent, but Elizabeth Siddal, Christina Rossetti, and William Michael Rossetti are buried in a family plot at Highgate Cemetery.

APPENDIX
CHRONOLOGY

The following timeline is offered as a brief reference guide to key events, works, and personalities associated with the Pre-Raphaelite Brotherhood. It is not intended as a comprehensive chronology, but rather as a sketch of significant dates—births and deaths, exhibitions, milestones, and historic events—that shaped the course of the movement. It may serve to orient the reader or supplement the fuller narrative presented in the preceding chapters.

—**1821 (April 16):** Birth of Ford Madox Brown in Calais, France. Though never an official PRB member, he becomes a mentor to the younger Pre-Raphaelites and adapts his style to their ideals.

—**1824 (January 8):** Birth of Wilkie Collins in Marylebone, London. A close friend of Charles Dickens and a pioneer of sensational fiction, he would later influence Pre-Raphaelite literary circles.

—**1827 (April 2):** Birth of William Holman Hunt in Cheapside, London. He would go on to co-found the Pre-Raphaelite Brotherhood and become known for his intensely spiritual and detailed paintings.

—**1828 (January 25):** Birth of Charles Allston Collins in Hampstead, London. A painter and writer, younger brother of Wilkie Collins, and a peripheral member of the Pre-Raphaelite circle.

—**1828 (May 12):** Birth of Dante Gabriel Rossetti in London. A poet-painter, he would go on to co-founds the Pre-Raphaelite Brotherhood, before influencing the Aesthetic movement.

—**1829 (June 8):** Birth of John Everett Millais in Southampton, England. A prodigy who entered the Royal Academy Schools at 11, he would go on to co-found the Pre-Raphaelite Brotherhood, later the foremost portrait painter of his age.

—**1830 (June 26):** Death of King George IV at Windsor Castle; he is succeeded by King William IV.

—**1830 (December 3):** Birth of Frederic Leighton in Scarborough, North Yorkshire. He would become a leading academic painter, closely associated with the Aesthetic Movement and later President of the Royal Academy.

—**1830 (December 5):** Birth of Christina Rossetti in Charlotte Street, London. She would become a renowned poet whose work (e.g. *Goblin Market*) is closely associated with the Pre-Raphaelite literary circle.

—**1833 (August 28):** Birth of Edward Burne-Jones in Birmingham. He would become a key second-generation Pre-Raphaelite painter, famed for his dreamlike medieval and mythological imagery.

—**1834 (March 24):** Birth of William Morris in Walthamstow, Essex (now London). An artist, poet, and designer, he later founded the Arts and Crafts movement.

—**1837 (April 5):** Birth of Algernon Charles Swinburne in London. A poet, he would come to exemplify the ideals of the Aesthetic Movement.

—**1837 (June 20):** Death of King William IV at Windsor Castle; he is succeeded by Queen Victoria.

—**1838 (June 28):** Coronation of Queen Victoria at Westminster Abbey.

—**1840 (February 10):** Marriage of Queen Victoria to Prince Albert of Saxe-Coburg and Gotha at the Chapel Royal of St James's Palace.

—**1841 (November 9):** Birth of Prince Albert Edward, later King Edward VII, at Buckingham Palace.

—**1848 (April 10):** John Ruskin marries Euphemia "Effie" Gray at Bowerswell House in Perth, Scotland. The marriage proves unhappy and remains unconsummated, leading to public scandal and eventual annulment.

—**1848 (September):** Founding of the PRB in London by Dante Gabriel Rossetti, William Holman Hunt, and John Everett Millais. They invite four others (James Collinson, Frederic G. Stephens, Thomas Woolner, and William Michael Rossetti) to join.

—1849 (April 6): Birth of John William Waterhouse in Rome, Italy. He would become associated with late Pre-Raphaelitism.

—1849 (March–May): First PRB works exhibited. Rossetti's *The Girlhood of Mary Virgin* is shown at the Free Exhibition. In May, Millais's and Hunt's PRB works are shown at the Royal Academy.

—1849: Elizabeth Siddal is discovered by the PRB, she would become the model and later muse and wife to Rossetti.

—1850 (January): Launch of *The Germ*, the Brotherhood's short-lived literary magazine promoting Pre-Raphaelite ideals.

—1850 (May): Millais exhibits *Christ in the House of His Parents*, prompting controversy and national attention.

—1850 (late): Internal tensions and departures (including Collinson) lead to the Brotherhood's quiet dissolution.

—1851 (May 1): Opening of the Great Exhibition in Hyde Park, London, showcasing industry and design from around the world.

—1851 (May): John Ruskin publicly defends the Pre-Raphaelites in *The Times*, greatly boosting their credibility.

—1851 (November): Rossetti and Siddal become engaged after a lengthy collaboration and courtship.

—**1852 (May):** Millais exhibits *Ophelia*, which becomes one of the most celebrated Pre-Raphaelite works. Elizabeth Siddal is the model.

—**1853 (November):** Millais is elected Associate of the Royal Academy, signaling institutional acceptance.

—**1854 (July 20):** Annulment of the marriage between John Ruskin and Effie Gray is granted by ecclesiastical court on grounds of non-consummation. The event causes a sensation in Victorian society and damages Ruskin's reputation.

—**1854:** Hunt completes *The Light of the World* and leaves for the Holy Land to paint biblical scenes in their historical setting.

—**1855 (July 3):** Millais marries Effie Gray, the former wife of John Ruskin.

—**1856:** Rossetti mentors William Morris and Edward Burne-Jones, persuading them to abandon clerical plans for art.

—**1857 (Summer):** Rossetti, Morris, and Burne-Jones decorate the Oxford Union with Arthurian murals. Morris meets Jane Burden.

—**1859 (April 26):** William Morris marries Jane Burden in Oxford, with Edward Burne-Jones as best man.

—**1859:** Red House, designed by Philip Webb and decorated by Morris and friends, is completed as a model of Arts and Crafts ideals.

—**1859 (November)**: Publication of Wilkie Collins's novel *The Woman in White*. The minor character of Professor Pesca is based on Rossetti's father, Gabriele Pasquale Rossetti.

—**1860 (May 23):** Rossetti marries Elizabeth Siddal in Hastings. He paints *Regina Cordium* to commemorate their union.

—**1860 (June):** Burne-Jones marries Georgiana Macdonald. Morris and Jane move into Red House.

—**1860 (July 17):** Charles Allston Collins marries Kate Dickens, daughter of Charles Dickens.

—**1861 (April 11):** Formation of Morris, Marshall, Faulkner & Co. The firm blends fine and decorative arts, bringing Pre-Raphaelite aesthetics to interior design.

—**1861 (December 14)**: Death of Prince Albert at Windsor Castle at age 42. The Queen's deep mourning impacts the national mood.

—**1862 (February 11):** Death of Elizabeth Siddal in London at age 32 from laudanum overdose. She is buried with Rossetti's manuscript of poems at Highgate Cemetery.

—**1862 (April):** Christina Rossetti publishes *Goblin Market and Other Poems*, her first volume of poetry, illustrated by Dante Gabriel Rossetti.

—**1865:** Swinburne publishes *Atalanta in Calydon*, a verse drama admired for its classical form and musicality.

—**1865 (December 28):** Hunt marries Fanny Waugh in London.

—**1866:** Swinburne releases *Poems and Ballads*, a controversial volume that draws attention for its erotic and pagan themes.

—**1865 (December 20):** Fanny Holman Hunt dies in Florence, Italy at the age of 33.

—**1869 (October):** Rossetti exhumes Siddal's coffin to retrieve his buried manuscript of poems.

—**1870 (April):** Rossetti publishes *Poems*, his first volume of poetry, which includes the first substantial version of *The House of Life*.

—**1870 (June 9):** Death of Charles Dickens in Gad's Hill Place, Kent, at age 58. Millais is invited to make a deathbed drawing of the author.

—**1871 (October):** Robert Buchanan attacks Rossetti in the *Contemporary Review*, launching the "fleshly school" controversy. Rossetti and Swinburne respond in print.

—**1873 (April 9):** Death of Charles Allston Collins in London at age 45.

—**1874:** Waterhouse begins exhibiting at the Royal Academy. His early work is classical in subject, later evolving toward a distinct Pre-Raphaelite style.

—**1875:** Morris dissolves the firm and reopens it as Morris & Co., taking full control.

—**1875 (November 8):** Hunt marries Edith Waugh, his late wife's sister, in Neuchâtel, Switzerland.

—**1877 (May):** Opening of the Grosvenor Gallery, where Burne-Jones exhibits major works and helps define the Aesthetic Movement.

—**1878:** Leighton is elected President of the Royal Academy, a post he will hold until his death.

—**1878 (November):** Whistler sues Ruskin for libel after Ruskin denounces his painting, *Nocturne in Black and Gold, the Falling Rocket*. Burne-Jones testifies for Ruskin. Whistler wins, but only nominal damages.

—**1879 (February):** Publication of *The Renaissance: Studies in Art and Poetry* by Walter Pater (revised edition). The book, influential among Aesthetes and younger artists, includes the famous "Conclusion" advocating the pursuit of intense experience and beauty.

—**1880:** Dante Gabriel Rossetti publishes *Ballads and Sonnets*, his second major poetry collection, which includes the completed sequence of *The House of Life*. It would be the last publication in his lifetime.

—**1882 (April 9):** Death of Dante Gabriel Rossetti in Birchington-on-Sea, Kent, at age 53. He is buried in the churchyard of All Saints, Birchington.

—**1883:** William Morris leases the Merton Abbey Works on the River Wandle in Surrey. This allows Morris & Co. to consolidate production of textiles, stained glass, and other decorative arts under one roof.

—**1884:** Edward Burne-Jones is elected an Associate of the Royal Academy. He will later decline full membership.

—**1888 (April):** J.W. Waterhouse exhibits *The Lady of Shalott* at the Royal Academy.

—**1889:** Waterhouse is elected a full member of the Royal Academy.

—**1889 (September 23):** Death of Wilkie Collins in London at age 65.

—**1891 (January):** Morris founds the Kelmscott Press, reviving hand-crafted book design.

—**1894 (January 25):** Death of Frederic Leighton in London at age 63, one day after receiving his peerage as Baron Leighton of Stretton.

—**1894 (December 29):** Death of Christina Rossetti in London at age 64.

—**1896 (May):** Publication of *The Works of Geoffrey Chaucer* printed by the Kelmscott Press. Designed by William Morris with illustrations by Edward Burne-Jones, the Kelmscott *Chaucer* is considered one of the finest examples of book-making in the private press movement.

—**1896 (August 13):** Death of John Everett Millais in London at age 67. He is interred at St. Paul's Cathedral.

—**1896 (October 3):** Death of William Morris at Kelmscott House, London, at age 62.

—**1898 (June 17):** Death of Edward Burne-Jones in London at age 64. He is later commemorated in Westminster Abbey.

—**1899 (July):** Publication of *The Life and Letters of Sir John Everett Millais* by his son John Guille Millais. The two-volume biography combines personal correspondence, reminiscences, and illustrations to document Millais's career.

—**1900 (January 20):** Death of John Ruskin in Brantwood, Cumbria, at age 80.

—**1900 (January 22):** Death of Queen Victoria at Osborne House, Isle of Wight, at age 81. She is succeeded by her son, King Edward VII.

—**1902 (August 9):** Coronation of King Edward VII at Westminster Abbey.

—**1905 (June):** Publication of *Pre-Raphaelitism and the Pre-Raphaelite Brotherhood* by William Holman Hunt. This two-volume work presents Hunt's detailed firsthand account of the Brotherhood's founding, aims, and history.

—**1909 (April 10):** Death of Algernon Charles Swinburne in London, at age 72.

—**1910 (May 6):** Death of King Edward VII at Buckingham Palace, London, at age 68. He is succeeded by his son, George V.

—**1910 (September 7):** Death of William Holman Hunt in London at age 83, the last surviving founder of the Brotherhood.

—**1914 (August 4):** Britain declares war on Germany, entering World War I. The war marks the definitive end of the world in which Pre-Raphaelitism and the Aesthetic Movement had flourished, and ushers in a new cultural and artistic era.

—**1917 (February 10):** Death of John William Waterhouse in London at age 67.

BIBLIOGRAPHY

CHAPTER ONE: P.R.B.

1. Hunt, William Holman. (1905) *Pre-Raphaelitism and the Pre-Raphaelite Brotherhood.* New York: The Macmillan Company, 82.

2. Hunt, *Pre-Raphaelitism*, 84.

3. Hunt, *Pre-Raphaelitism*, 83.

4. Hunt, *Pre-Raphaelitism*, 84.

5. La Sizeranne, Robert de; Byrd, Andrew (trans). (2008) *The Pre-Raphaelites.* New York: Parkstone Press, 7.

6. Hunt, *Pre-Raphaelitism*, ix.

7. Hunt, *Pre-Raphaelitism*, 105-106.

8. Hunt, *Pre-Raphaelitism*, 107.

9. Rossetti, Dante Gabriel; Rossetti, William Michael (ed). (1895) *Dante Gabriel Rossetti: His Family-Letters with a Memoir.* London: Ellis and Elvey, 135.

10. Rossetti, William Michael. (1906) *Some Reminiscences of William Michael Rossetti.* New York: Charles Scribner's Sons, 71.

11. Rossetti, *His Family-Letters*, 128.

12. Jacobi, Carol. (2012) "Sugar, Salt and Curdled Milk: Millais and the Synthetic Subject," *Tate Papers 18.*

13. Reach, Angus. (May 4, 1850) "Town and Table Talk," *The Illustrated London News.* Reprinted in: Ghose, Sudhindra Nath. (1929) *Dante Gabriel Rossetti & Contemporary Criticism, 1849-1882.* Dijon: Imprimerie Darantière, 34.

14. Dickens, Charles. (June 15, 1850) "Old Lamps for New," *Household Word.* London: Ward, Lock, and Tyler, 1:265.

15. Dickens, *Household Words*, 265-266.

16. Dickens, *Household Words*, 266.

17. Nath, *Dante Gabriel Rossetti & Contemporary Criticism*, 34.

18. Quoted in: Bronkhurst, Judith. (2006) *William Holman Hunt: A Catalogue Raisonné.* New Haven: Yale University Press, 134-136.

19. Hunt, *Pre-Raphaelitism*, 190.

20. Rossetti, *His Family-Letters*, 160.

21. Hunt, *Pre-Raphaelitism*, 53.

22. Hunt, *Pre-Raphaelitism*, 276-277.

23. Hunt, *Pre-Raphaelitism*, 277.

24. Hunt, *Pre-Raphaelitism*, 278.

25. Packer, Lona Mosk. (1963) *Christina Rossetti*. Berkeley: University of California Press, 17.

26. Rossetti, William Michael (ed). (1901) *The Germ: Thoughts towards Nature in Poetry, Literature and Art, Being a Facsimile Reprint of the Literary Organ of the Pre-Raphaelite Brotherhood, Published in 1850*. London: Eliot Stock, 20.

27. Rossetti, *The Germ*, 50.

28. Rossetti, *The Germ*, 67.

29. Tennyson, Alfred. (1830) *Poems, Chiefly Lyrical*. London: Effingham Wilson, 30.

30. Tennyson, Hallam. (1897) *Alfred Lord Tennyson: A Memoir by His Son (Volume 1)*. London, Macmillan and Co., 166.

31. Coleridge, Samuel Taylor. (1836) *Specimens of the Table Talk of Samuel Taylor Coleridge*. London: John Murray, 273.

32. Byron, George Gordon. (1847) *The Poetical Works of Lord Byron Complete in One Volume*. London: John Murray, 2.

33. Tennyson, Hallam. (1899) *Alfred Lord Tenyson: A Memoir by His Son (Volume 3)*, Leipzig: Bernhard Tauchnitz, 118.

34. Tennyson, *Alfred Lord Tenyson: A Memoir by His Son*, 1:194.

35. Tennyson, *Alfred Lord Tenyson: A Memoir by His Son*, 3:112.

36. Tennyson, *Alfred Lord Tenyson: A Memoir by His Son*, 3:112-113.

37. Quoted in Tennyson, Alfred; Ricks, Christopher (ed). (1987) *The Poems of Tennyson*. London: Longman, 1:387.

38. Tennyson, *Alfred Lord Tenyson: A Memoir by His Son*, 1:117.

39. Tennyon, Alfed. (1872) *The Poetical Works of Alfred Lord Tennyson*. Boston, James R. Osgood and Company, 54.

40. Tennyson, *The Poetical Works*, 58.

41. Tennyson, Alfred; Tennyson, Hallam (ed). (1908) *Idylls of the King*. Macmillan and Co., 406.

42. Tennyson, *Idylls of the King*, 418.

43. Rossetti, Dante Gabriel; Rossetti, William Michael (ed). (1887) *The Collected Works of Dante Gabriel Rossetti in Two Volumes*. London: Ellis and Elvey, 503.

44. Nath, *Dante Gabriel Rossetti & Contemporary Criticism*, 45.

45. Ruskin, John. (1861) *Modern Painters*. New York: John Wiley, 1:21.

46. Ruskin, *Modern Painters*, 413.

47. Mumby, Frank Arthur (ed). (1906) *Letters of Literary Men: The Nineteenth Century*. New York: George Routledge & Sons, 607-608.

48. Nath, *Dante Gabriel Rossetti & Contemporary Criticism*, 47.

49. Ruskin, John. (1894) *The Stones of Venice*. New York: Bryan, Taylor & Company, 2:203.

50. Willsdon, Clare. (2000) *Mural Painting in Britain 1840-1940*. Oxford: Oxford University Press, 30.

51. Atterbury, Paul. (1995) *A.W.N. Pugin: Master of Gothic Revival*. New Haven and London: Yale University Press, 223.

52. Auerbach, Jeffey A. (1999) *The Great Exhibition of 1851: A Nation on Display*. New Haven and London: Yale University Press, 116.

53. The Queen's Gallery became The King's Gallery at the accession of HM King Charles III.

54. Frith, William Powell. (1889) *My Autobiography and Reminiscences*. London: Richard Bentley and Son, 172.

55. Remington, Vanessa. (2012) "Queen Victoria, Prince Albert and their relations with artists," in *Victoria & Albert: Art & Love, Essays from a study day held at the National Gallery*, https://www.royalcollection.org.uk/collection/themes/exhibitions/victoria-albert-art-love/the-queens-gallery-bucking ham-palace/contents

56. Panton, Jane Ellen. (1908) *Leaves from a Life*. London: George Bell & Sons, 40

57. Remington, "Queen Victoria, Prince Albert and their relations with artists."

58. Jones, Kathryn. (2012) "'To wed high art with mechanical skill': Prince Albert and the industry of art," in *Victoria & Albert: Art & Love, Essays from a study day held at the National Gallery*, https://www.royalcollection.org.uk/collection/themes/exhibitions/victoria-albert-art-love/the-queens-gallery-buckingham-palace/contents

59. Kharibian, Leah. (2010) *Passionate Patrons: Victoria & Albert and the Arts*. London: Royal Collection, 6.

60. Shakespeare, William. (1603) *Hamlet, Prince of Denmark*. In G. B. Harrison (Ed.), *The Tragedy of Hamlet*. London: Penguin Books, 1937. Act IV, Scene VII.

61. Hunt, *Pre-Raphaelitism*, 338.

62. Fleming, Gordon H. (1998) *John Everett Millais: A Biography*. London: Constable and Co., 64.

63. ibid.

64. Millais, John Guille. (1899) *The Life and Letters of Sir John Everett Millais*. London: Methuen & Co., 1:249.

CHAPTER TWO: THE MUSE

1. Rossetti, Dante Gabriel; Hill, George Birbeck (ed). (1897) *Letters of Dante Gabriel Rossetti to William Allingham, 1854-1870*. London: T. Fisher Unwin, 144.

2. Rossetti, Dante Gabriel; Wahl, John Robert (ed); Doughty, Oswald (ed). (1965) *Letters of Dante Gabriel Rossetti: 1835-1860*. Oxford: The Clarendon Press, 65.

3. Orlando, Emily J. (2012) "Visual Arts," in Rattray, Laura (ed). *Edith Wharton in Context*. Cambridge: Cambridge University Press, 184.

4. MacCarthy, Fiona. (2012) *The Last Pre-Raphaelite: Edward Burne-Jones and the Victorian Imagination*. Cambridge: Harvard University Press, 83.

5. Hunt, *Pre-Raphaelitism*, 198-199.

6. Chatfield, Stephanie. (10 January 2012) "Pre-Raphaelite Marriages: Dante Gabriel Rossetti and Elizabeth Siddal," *Pre-Raphaelite Sisterhood*. https://preraphaelitesisterhood.com/pre-raphaelite-marriages-dante-gabriel-rossetti-and-elizabeth-siddal/

7. Millais, *Life and Letters*, 1:144.

8. Rossetti, William Michael (ed). (1899) *Ruskin: Rossetti: Preraphaelitism, Papers 1854 to 1862*. London: George Allen, 33.

9. Anthony, P.D. (1983) *John Ruskin's Labour: A Study of Ruskin's Social Theory*. Cambridge: Cambridge University Press, 46.

10. Shrimpton, Nicholas. (2015) "Politics and economics," in O'Gorman, Francis. *The Cambridge Companion to John Ruskin*. Cambridge: Cambridge University Press, 117.

11. ibid.

12. Anthony, *John Ruskin's Labour*, 45-46.

13 O'Goman, *The Cambridge Companion to John Ruskin*, 117.

14. Anthony, *John Ruskin's Labour*, 10.

15. Chatfield, Stephanie. (16 January 2012) "Pre-Raphaelite Marriage: Ruskin, Effie and Millais," *Pre-Raphaelite Sisterhood*. https://preraphaelitesisterhood.com/pre-raphaelite-marriage-ruskin-effie-and-millais/

16. Hilton, Tim. (2002) *John Ruskin*. New Haven and London: Yale University Press, 118.

17. Fleming, Gordon H. (1967) *Rossetti and the Pre-Raphaelite Brotherhood*. London: Hart Davies, 208.

18. Hilton, *John Ruskin*, 186.

19. Cooper, Suzanne Fagence. (2010) *Effie: The Passionate Lives of Effie Gray, John Ruskin and John Everett Millais*. New York: St. Martin's Press, 5.

20. ibid.

21. Cooper, *Effie*, 6.

22. Lutyens, Mary. (1967) *Millais and the Ruskins*. London: John Murray, 230.

23. Campbell-Johnson, Rachel. (23 August 2014) "Ruskin, Millais and Euphemia Gray: a very Victorian scandal," in *The Times*.

24. Millais, *Life and Letters*, 1:287-288.

25. Potter, Beatrix; Linder, Leslie (ed). (1966) *The Journal of Beatrix Potter from 1881 to 1899*. London: Frederick Warne & Co., 418.

26. Cooper, *Effie*, 6.

27. Woolner, Thomas; Woolner, Amy. (1917) *Thomas Woolner, R.A., Sculptor and Poet: His Life in Letters*. London: Chapman and Hall, Ltd., 159.

28. Holloway, Julia Bolton. (2024) *Florence's English Cemetery, 1827-1877: Thunders of White Silence*. Newcastle upon Tyne: Cambridge Scholars Publishing, 174-175.

29. Marsh, Jan. (1999) *Dante Gabriel Rossetti: Painter and Poet*. London: Weidenfeld & Nicolson, 42.

30. James, Henry. (20 June 1869) "Letter to John La Farge." Manuscript. New York: The New-York Historical Society, La Farge Papers, ms 360.

31. Moyle, Franny. (2009) Desperate Romantics: The Private Lives of the Pre-Raphaelites. London: John Murray, 195.

32. Rossetti, *Letters of Dante Gabriel Rossetti: 1835-1860*, 760-761.

33. Rossetti, *His Family-Letters*, 171.

34. Burne-Jones, Georgiana. (1904) *Memorials of Edward Burne-Jones*. New York and London: The Macmillan Company, 208.

35. James, Henry; Lubbock, Percy (ed). (1920) *The Letters of Henry James*. New York: Charles Scribner's Sons, 1:17-18.

36. Stoker, Bram. (1897) *Dracula*. London: Archibald Constable and Company, Chapter 11.

37. Trumble, Angus. (10 January 2019) "'O Uommibatto' How the Pre-Raphaelites Became Obsessed with the Wombat," in *The Public Domain Review*. https://publicdomainreview.org/essay/o-uommibatto-how-the-pre-raphaelites-became-obsessed-with-the-wombat/

38. ibid.

39. Louras, Nick. (2003) "Wombats and Dante Gabriel Rossetti," in *The Chelsea Society Annual Report*. London: The Chelsea Society, 41.

40. Wood, Christopher. (1981) *The Pre-Raphaelites*. New York: The Viking Press,148.

41. Trippi, Peter. (2003) "John William Waterhouse," in *Pre-Raphaelite and Other Masters: The Andrew Lloyd Webber Collection*. London: The Royal Academy of Arts, 126.

42. Baker, James K.; Baker, Kathy L. (Fall 1999) "Miss Muriel Foster: The John William Waterhouse Model," in *The Journal of Pre-Raphaelite Studies*. New Series 8. See also: Baker, James K.; Baker, Kathy L. (2004) "The *Lamia* in the Art of John William Waterhouse," in *The British Art Journal*. Vol V, No 2.

43. Rossetti, Dante Gabriel. (1913) The Poetical Works of Dante Gabriel Rossetti. Boston: Little, Brown, and Company, 2:136.

CHAPTER THREE: SECRET GARDEN

1. Anonymous. (2017) "Victorians: Landscape," *English Heritage*. http://www.english-heritage.org.uk/learn/story-of-england/victorian/landscape/

2. ibid.

3. Endersby, Jim. (July 25, 2014) "How botanical gardens helped to establish

the British Empire," *Financial Times*. https://www.ft.com/content/dcd33 da0-0e69-11e4-a1ae-00144feabdc0

4. ibid.

5. Tipping, H. Avray. (1929) "The Garden of Pleasure in England from Plantagenet to Victorian Times," *Journal of the Royal Horticultural Society,* Vol. LIV; Part II.

6. Gerrish, Helena. (September 1, 2016) "Edwardian Garden Style," *The English Garden.* http://www.theenglishgarden.co.uk/expert-advice/design-solutions/design-edwardian-garden-style/

7. *English Heritage*, "Victorians: Landscape."

8. Morris, William. (1875) *The Defence of Guenevere and Other Poems*. London: Ellis & White, 6.

9. Rossetti, Christina; Crump, RW (ed). (1979) *The Complete Poems of Christina Rossetti*. Baton Rouge: Louisiana State University Press, 56.

10. Roe, Dinah. (Spring 2019) "Naturally Artificial: The Pre-Raphaelite Garden Enclosed," *Victorian Poetry*. Volume 57, Number 1, 131-153.

11. ibid.

12. Aksich, Caroline. (March 29, 2014) "The Flowers of Middlemarch: Dorothea Brooke, Rosamond Vincy and Mary Garth." https://www.carolineaksich.com/book-babble/2014/3/29/the-flowers-of-middlemarch-dorothea-brooke-rosamond-vincy-and-mary-garth

13. Herrick, Robert. (1898) *Works of Robert Herrick (Vol. 1): Hesperides & Noble Numbers*. London: Lawrence & Bullen, 102.

14. Stephens, Frederic George. (1860) *William Holman Hunt and His Works: A Memoir of the Artist's Life, with Description of His Pictures*. London: James Nisbet & Co., 34.

15. ibid.

16. Shakespeare, *Hamlet*, Act IV, Scene V.

17. Chatfield, Stephanie. (May 28, 2014) "Ophelia's Flowers," *The Pre-Raphaelite Sisterhood*. https://preraphaelitesisterhood.com/ophelias-flowers/

18. Grabau, Lydia. (February 20, 2013) "Ophelia's Flowers," *Hamlet Dramaturgy*. https://hamletdramaturgy.wordpress.com/2013/02/20/ophelias-flowers/

19. Shakespeare, *Hamlet*, Act IV, Scene VII.

20. Millais, *Life and Letters*, 1:145.

21. Phythian, John Ernest. (1911) *Millais*. London: George Allen & Company, Ltd., 46.

22. Anonymous. (May 1, 1852) "Exhibition of the Royal Academy," *The Times* (London). Number 21104.

23. Søndergaard, Peter Brix. (2018) "'Something strangely perverse'. Nature and Gender in J. E. Millais's *Ophelia*," *Romantik: Journal for the Study of Romanticisms*. Volume 7, Number 1.

24. Burnett, Frances Hodgson. (1911) *The Secret Garden*. New York: Frederick A. Stokes.

25. Gohlke, Madelon S. (April, 1980) "Re-Reading the Secret Garden," *College English*. Volume 41, Number 8.

CHAPTER FOUR: DEATH AND RESURRECTION

1. Hunt, *Pre-Raphaelitism*, 159.

2. ibid.

3. Hunt, *Pre-Raphaelitism*, 160.

4. ibid.

5. Ezekiel 37:1-12.

6. Corinthians 15:52.

7. Corinthians 15:16.

8. Jurgens, W.A. (1970-1979) *The Faith of the Early Fathers*. Collegeville: The Liturgical Press, 1:63.

9. Jurgens, *The Faith of the Early Fathers*, 1:73.

10. Jurgens, *The Faith of the Early Fathers*, 1:85.

11. Jurgens, *The Faith of the Early Fathers*, 1:150.

12. Jurgens, *The Faith of the Early Fathes*, 3:107.

13. Wright, N.T. (2011) *Revelation For Everyone*. Louisville: Westminster John Knox Press, 185.

14. Luther, Martin; Pelikan, Jaroslav (ed); Hilton, Oswald (ed). (1964) *Luther's Works: Volume 4*. Saint Louis: Concordia Publishing House, 190.

15. Cranmer, Thomas; Cox, John Edmund (ed). (1844) *Writings and Disputations of Thomas Cranmer, Archibishop of Canterbury, Martyr, 1556, Relative to the Sacrament of the Lord's Supper*. Cambridge: The Parker Society / The University Press, 177.

16. ibid.

17. Mohler, R. Albert, Jr. (April 7, 2006) "Do Christians Still Believe in the Resurrection of the Body?" https://albertmohler.com/2006/04/07/do-christians-still-believe-in-the-resurrection-of-the-body/

18. Kenny, Anthony. (2007) *A New History of Western Philosophy in Four Parts*. Oxford: Oxford University Press.

19. Van Biema, Dan; Wright, N.T. (February 7, 2008) "Christians Wrong About Heaven, Says Bishop," *Time*. https://time.com/archive/6942509/christians-wrong-about-heaven-says-bishop/

20. Middleton, J. Richard. (2014) *A New Heaven and a New Earth: Reclaiming Biblical Eschatology*. Grand Rapids: Baker Academic.

21. Revelation 22:1-2.

22. Revelation 21:24.

23. Bradley, Ian. (2023) *Breathers of an Ampler Day: Victorian Views of Heaven.* Durham: Sacristy Press, 33.

24. Castle, Brian. (1994) *Sing a New Song to the Lord.* London: Darton, Longman & Todd, 35.

25. Darlington, James (ed). (1899) *The Hymnal of the Church, Adopted by the General Convention of the Protestant Episcopal Church in the United States of America in the Year of Our Lord Eighteen Hundred and Ninety-*Two. New York: Thomas Whittaker, 190.

26. Darlington, *The Hymnal of the Church,* 95-96.

27. Various. (1897) *Report of the Sub-Committee on Hymns on Heaven and Kindred Subjects.* Norwich: Hymns Ancient & Modern. See also: Bradley, *Breathers of an Ampler Day,* 32-33.

28. Rossetti, *Some Reminiscences of William Michael Rossetti,* 119-120.

29. Benson, Arthur C. (1904) *Rossetti.* London: Macmillan & Co., 6.

30. Benson, *Rossetti,* 6-7.

31. Kooistra, Lorraine Janzen. (2002) *Christina Rossetti and Illustration: A Publishing History.* Athens: Ohio University Press, 29.

32. Mégroz, Rodolphe Louis. (1928) *Dante Gabriel Rossetti: Painter Poet of Heaven in Earth.* London: Faber & Gwyer, 26.

33. Mason, Emma. (2018) *Christina Rossetti: Poetry, Ecology, Faith.* Oxford: Oxford University Press.

34. Burrows, Henry William (ed). (1855) *Hymns for Use in the Church.* London: William Skeffington.

35. Rossetti, Christina. (1892) *The Face of the Deep: A Devotional Commentary on the Apocalypse.* London: Society for Promoting Christian Knowledge, 467.

36. Rossetti, Christina. (1902) *Times Flies: A Reading Diary.* London: Society for Promoting Christian Knowledge, 128.

37. Bell, Mackenzie. (1898) *Christina Rossetti: A Biographical and Critical Study.* London: Thomas Burleigh, 98.

38. Rossetti, Christina; Rossetti, William Michael (ed). (1904) *Poems of Christina Rossetti, Chosen and Edited by William M. Rossetti.* London: Macmillan and Co., ix.

39. Bradley, *Breathers of an Ampler Day,* 67.

40. Bell, *Christina Rossetti,* 211.

41. Rossetti, *Time Flies,* 88.

42. Sampson, John (ed). (1905) *The Poetical Works of William Blake: A New and Verbatim Text From the Manuscript Engraved and Letterpress Orginals with Variorum Readings and Bibliographical Notes and Prefaces.* 138-139.

43. Butlin, Matin. (December 15, 1968) "William Rossetti's Annotations to Gilchrist's Life of William Blake," *Blake: An Illustrated Quarterly.* Volume 2, Issue 3.

44. Bassalik-de Vries, Johanna Christina Emerentia. (1911) *Blake in his Relation*

to Dante Gabriel Rossetti: A Dissertation presented to the Philosophical Faculty of the University of Zurich for the Acquisition of the Degree of Doctor of Philosophy. Basel: Buchdruckerei Brin & Cie., 6.

45. Rossetti, *Poems of Christina Rossetti*, 229.

46. Revelation 20:13.

47. Hammerschlag, Keren Rosa. (2015) *Frederic Leighton: Death, Mortality, Resurrection*. Abingdon: Ashgate Publishing, 176.

48. Anonymous. (January 23, 1891) "Decorations at St. Paul's Cathedral," *The Building News and Engineering Journal*. Volume LX, Number 1881.

49. Hammerschlag, *Frederic Leighton*, 175.

50. Hammerschlag, *Frederic Leighton*, 177.

51. Rossetti, Dante Gabriel. (1898) *The Blessed Damozel, as First Written by Dante Gabriel Rossetti and Published in "The Germ" in 1850*. New York: M.F. Mansfield, xiv.

52. Rossetti, *The Blessed Damozel*, xix.

53. Rossetti, *The Blessed Damozel*, v.

54. Wright, "Christians Wrong About Heaven, Says Bishop," *Time*.

55. Riede, David G. (1983) *Dante Gabriel Rossetti and the Limits of Victorian Vision*. Ithaca: Cornell University Press, 111.

56. Riede, *Dante Gabriel Rossetti*, 111-112.

57. Rossetti, *His Family-Letters*, 114.

CHAPTER FIVE: TWILIGHT OF THE GODS

1. Weinreb, Ben; Hibbert, Christopher; Keay, Julia; Keay, John. (2011) *The London Encyclopaedia*. London: Macmillan, 162.

2. Buchanan, Robert. (1872) *The Fleshly School of Poetry, and Other Phenomena of the Day*. London: Strahan & Co. See also: Rossetti, Dante Gabriel. (December 16, 1871) "The Stealthy School of Criticism," *Athenaeum*. No 2303.

3. Hubbard, Elbert. (1906) *Little Journeys to the Homes of Great Lovers: Dante Gabriel Rossetti and Elizabeth Siddal*. East Aurora: The Roycrofters, 22.

4. Rossetti, *His Family-Letters*, 390-393.

5. Rossetti, Dante; Fredeman, William (ed). (2010) *The Correspondence of Dante Gabriel Rossetti*. Cambridge: D.S. Brewer, IX:680.

6. Anonymous. (April 11, 1882) "The death of Mr. D.G. Rossetti," published in *The Guardian*. https://www.theguardian.com/theguardian/2011/apr/11/archive-the-death-of-mr-d-g-rossetti-1882

7. Wilson, David Alec; MacArthur, David Wilson. (1934) *Carlyle in Old Age (1865-1881)*. London: Kegan Paul, Trench, Trubner & Co., 406.

8. Van Gogh, Vincent. (1927) *The Letters of Vincent Van Gogh to His Brother, 1872-1886*. London: Constable & Co., 374.

9. Lepine, Ayla. (2017) "Anglican Art and Architecture, *c.*1837-1914," in Strong, Rowan (ed). *The Oxford History of Anglicanism, Volume III: Partisan Anglicanism and its Global Expansion, 1829-1914*. Oxford: Oxford University Press, 405.

10. Gere, Charlotte; Munn, Geoffrey C. (1989) *Artists' Jewelry: Pre-Raphaelite to Arts and Crafts*. Woodbridge: Antique Collectors' Club, 63.

CHAPTER SIX: THE WHEEL OF FORTUNE

1. Monahan, Patrick. (December 31, 2022) "The Return of *Flaming June*: Once derided as an eyesore, Victorian painting is roaring back on both sides of the Atlantic," *Air Mail*. https://airmail.news/arts-intel/highlights/the-return-of-flaming-june-1109

2. De Wolfe, Elsie. (1914) *The House in Good Taste*. New York: The Century Co., 48.

3. Christie, Agatha. (1964) *A Caribbean Mystery*. London: Collins Crime Club.

4. Christie, Agatha. (1939) *The Regatta Mystery and Other Stories*. New York: Dodd, Mead and Company.

5. Walker, Kirsty Stonell. (May 27, 2017) "Hopelessly Vieux Jeu!," *The Kissed Mouth*. https://fannycornforth.blogspot.com/2017/05/hopelessly-vieux-jeu.html

6. Barringer, Tim. (Spring 2006) "Victorian Culture and the Museum: Before and After the White Cube," *Journal of Victorian Culture*. Volume 11, Number 1.

7. Anonymous. (January 11, 2009) "(Obituary) Christopher Wood: flamboyant art dealer and prolific author," *The Times*. London.

8. Kennedy, Maeve. (June 20, 2016) "Leighton's Flaming June to go on display in studio where it was painted," *The Guardian*. https://www.theguardian.com/artanddesign/2016/jun/20/flaming-june-frederic-lord-leighton-house-museum

9. Barker, Nicolas. (January 31, 1997) "Obituary: Jeremy Maas," *The Independent*. https://www.independent.co.uk/news/people/obituary-jeremy-maas-1286047.html

10. Ash, Russel. (1989) *Top Ten of Everything*. London: Queen Anne Press, 100.

11. Barringer, "Victorian Culture and the Museum: Before and After the White Cube." See also: Hayman, Pete. (March 29, 2011) "Architect selected for V&A museum revamp," *CLADnews*. https://www.cladglobal.com/architecture_design_news?codeid=250803

12. Matson, Lisa Dallape. (2010) *Representations of Dante Gabriel Rossetti: Portrayals in Fiction, Drama, Music, and Film*. Amherst: Cambria Press, 120.